D0472594

"If you're not already familiar with Emily's genius kitchen talent, you'd better grab copies of all her books. Her recipes are delicious and her photography is stunning!"

—*HEATHER PACE*, author of *Sweetly Raw*

"Emily's food is beautiful and vibrant and really showcases her love for real, wholesome ingredients. Her book is a must for anyone wanting to create mouthwatering, nourishing meals in the kitchen."

— *CHRIS ANCA*, creator of talesofakitchen.com

"Emily concocts the most stunning, healthy and heartfelt food around. With every flip of the page I'm more and more inspired."

—*SOPHIE MACKENZIE*, creator of wholeheartedeats.com

"The very first book I bought after becoming a vegan was Emily's. Thanks to her, my very first attempt at a raw vegan dessert was a resounding success. Her fun, creative and wholesome cooking is delicious and inspirational."

—*MAYA SOZER*, creator of dreamyleaf.com

"Emily's cookbooks are a beautiful extension of the creativity and vibrant raw food masterpieces on her blog. Now that she's added cooked food to her repertoire, she's pretty much unstoppable. I'm so happy to have this beautifully photographed cookbook on my shelf!"

—*AMBER ST. PETER*, creator of fettlevegan.com

"You know that if one of Emily's recipes tastes even half as good as it looks, you're in for a pretty grand treat. Whole, delicious plant ingredients are gloriously celebrated, as they deserve to be, in each and every one of these recipes. Thanks for another gem, Em!"

—*EMMA SMITH*, owner & founder of Zimt Artisan Chocolates Ltd.

"*The Rawsome Vegan Cookbook* is the perfect guide to incorporating nutrient-dense whole foods into your diet with recipes that are enticing and soul-satisfying. As you eat the book with your eyes, be prepared for mouth-watering and immediate cravings."

—*COLIN MEDHURST*, co-founder of Feed Life

the RAWSOME
VEGAN COOKBOOK

A BALANCE OF RAW AND LIGHTLY-COOKED, GLUTEN-FREE PLANT-BASED MEALS FOR HEALTHY LIVING

EMILY von EUW

Bestselling author of *Rawsome Vegan Baking* and *100 Best Juices, Smoothies and Healthy Snacks*, and creator of the blog This Rawsome Vegan Life

PAGE STREET
PUBLISHING CO.

PAGE STREET
PUBLISHING CO.

Copyright © 2015 Emily von Euw

First published in 2015 by
Page Street Publishing Co.
27 Congress Street, Suite 105
Salem, MA 01970
www.pagestreetpublishing.com

Distributed by Macmillan, sales in Canada by The Canadian Manda Group.

18   17   3 4 5

ISBN-13: 978-1-62414-171-3
ISBN-10: 1-62414-171-4

Library of Congress Control Number: 2015947373

Cover and book design by Page Street Publishing Co.

Printed and bound in China.

Page Street is proud to be a member of 1% for the Planet. Members donate one percent of their sales to one or more of the over 1,500 environmental and sustainability charities across the globe who participate in this program.

*This book
is dedicated
to you.*

CONTENTS

WELCOME - 10

RAW - 14

Carrot Daikon Salad with Lemon Juice + Basil — 44

Arugula Leaves with Golden Beet, Kiwi, Radish + Orange Juice Dressing — 47

Garlic-Marinated Morel Mushrooms with Heirloom Tomato, Basil Sauce, Radish + Dill — 48

Radish Greens with Cilantro, Lemon, Snap Peas + Avocado — 51

King Oyster Mushrooms Layered with Heirloom Tomato, Basil + Avocado — 52

Sweet Corn Quiche with Buckwheat Onion Crust + Cherry Tomatoes — 55

Kale Salad with Carrot, Pineapple + Coconut Sauce — 56

Pho Bowl with Basil, Mint, Chives, Bok Choy + Leeks — 59

Som Tam: Green Papaya Salad — 60

Get Your Greenz: Leafy Salad with Green Onions, Zucchini Strips, Purple Cabbage
+ Tangy Tahini Dressing — 63

Raw Tacos with Sweet Corn, Kiwi, Cumin-Marinated Tomatoes + Pea Shoots — 64

Shaved Fennel with Grapefruit, Avocado + Radishes — 67

Stuffed Tomatoes with Carrot-Cauliflower Filling — 68

Radicchio Salad with Parsley, Sunflower Seeds, Carrot + Spirulina Dressing — 71

Lettuce, Sorrel, Pea Greens, Fava Greens, Tomatoes, Shredded Veg + Thick Parsley Dressing — 72

Massaged Green Salad with Creamy Purple Dressing + Cucumber — 75

Green Coconut Curry with Marinated 'Shrooms, Broccoli + Tomato — 76

Beet Ravioli with Almond Thyme Pâté + Basil — 79

Lasagna: Zucchini Noodles, Heirloom Tomato, Sweet Corn + Brazil Nut Cheeze — 80

Quick Tomato Soup with Miso + Thyme — 83

Spicy Noodle Bowl with Beet, Carrot, Zucchini + Sweet Tamarind Sauce — 84

Sweet Corn, Baby Tomato + Chimichurri Mix Up — 87

Tomato Stacks with Avocado, Corn + Spices — 88

Farmer's Market Bounty: Mixed Greens with Garlic Shoots, Baby Tomatoes, Green Onions, Golden Beets
+ Lemony Ginger Dressing — 91

Broccoli Pesto with Swiss Chard, Sliced Asparagus, Radish, Beets + Sunflower Seeds — 92

Onion Corn Bread Sandwich with Avocado + Spinach Filling — 95

COOKED - 96

Mac + Cheeze: The Healthy Way — 99

The Green Bowl: Steamed Broccoli, Green Lentils, Baked Zucchini + Basil Pesto — 100

I Love Yu Choy: Steamed Greens with Brown Rice, Beets, Black Beans + Ginger Almond Sauce — 103

Soba Noodles with Avocado, Carrot Ribbons, Shredded Spinach + Maple Miso Glaze — 104

Pumpkin Soup with Potatoes, Pumpkin Seeds, Leeks + Coconut Milk — 107

Jasmine Rice with Edamame, Black Beans + Salsa — 108

Sweet Potato Slices with Lime-Spritzed Baby Greens + Corn — 110

Creamy Cauliflower Sauce with Rice Noodles — 111

Sautéed Asparagus with Marinated Mushrooms + Almonds — 113

Baked Eggplant with Rosemary Salt, Savory + Cilantro Sauce — 114

Warming Miso Soup with Leeks + Ginger — 117

Baked Yams with Quinoa, Sprouts, Spicy Tofu + Chili Almond Sauce — 118

Cream of Carrot Soup with Fennel Seed, Paprika + Thyme — 121

Creamy Butternut Squash with Sage, Cranberry Jam + Micro Greens — 122

My Fave Dinner: Sweet Potato with Tahini, Lemon + Black Pepper — 125

Winter Melon Soup with Ginger, Cilantro + Shimeji Mushrooms — 126

Rice Noodles with Peas, Mint, Basil + Peanut Lime Sauce — 129

Ramen Noodles with Baby Bok Choy, Fresh Turmeric + Ginger Broth — 130

Tricolor Quinoa with Tahini, Steamed Beets, Carrots + Peas — 133

Sweet + Sour Bok Choy with Whole-Grain Miso Noodles — 134

Red Kuri Squash with Basmati Rice + Baby Spinach Tossed in Ginger Lemon Dressing — 137

Peas + Greens: Paprika-Baked Yams with Spinach, Peas — 138

Whole Food Proteins: Baked Potatoes with Golden Beets, Tahini Greens + White Navy Beans — 141

One-Pot Veggie Noodle Soup with Miso Broth — 142

Steamed Asparagus with Red Rice, Mushrooms, Nori + Thick Tomato Sauce — 145

Acorn Squash with Romanesco Broccoli + Creamy Ginger Almond Gravy — 146

RESOURCES - 178

WELCOME

EAT PLANTS

This book is about finding happiness by eating plants. I believe health is the foundation for high-quality living, and when we have the ability to live well, we can achieve bliss! Think about it this way: we are alive because of our bodies—we exist and live through them—so doesn't it make sense to keep your body (i.e., the vehicle that lets you experience the world) in the best shape possible? Heck yeah, it does.

How do we do that? By eating plants. Although there's never-ending debate out there about what the perfect diet is or isn't, pretty much everyone agrees that an eating plan full of fruits and vegetables is a good one. Check out my resources section for more information on this. Being healthy makes me happy, so I eat plants.

The cookbook you're holding is mainly split into two chapters: raw and cooked recipes. I love both these kinds of eating; raw recipes are hydrating, light and colorful while cooked foods are grounding, nourishing and hearty. A diet that's a balance of both is definitely gonna make ya feel good. Real good.

By basing your diet around the edible plant kingdom, you're making an environmentally responsible choice. A whole foods, plant-based diet produces the least greenhouse gas emissions and requires the least water and land usage compared to all others. Freaky fact: animal agriculture produces more greenhouse emissions than all transportation combined, according to the Food and Agriculture Organization of the United Nations. Yikes. Go for the Yam Burger (page 26) instead of the hamburger. Eating a diet that is easy on the earth makes me happy, so I eat plants.

Finally, going vegan is the ethical decision. No matter how delicious bacon might taste, somebody had to die for it to be created. That makes me feel uncomfortable, so I don't consume bacon or any other food product that necessarily involves pain and death. We just don't need to eat that stuff, and I'd rather hug my animal friends than eat them. Being kind and compassionate to others makes me happy, so I eat plants.

You don't have to agree with anything I just said. But if you like delicious food, then you're still gonna dig what's in this cookbook. LET'S EAT SOME PLANTS.

TIPS

Buy organic, locally grown produce (aka, the best food around). Check out the farmer's market nearest to you and stock up every week. On average, it costs about the same as the grocery store, but the tastes, colors and textures are incomparable. You cannot make good recipes unless you start with good ingredients.

Don't worry about following my recipes exactly—go with the flow and add your own zesty infusions (figuratively and literally, 'cause lemon zest makes everything better anyway). It's fun to play around with amounts, spices and methods and tweak to your personal preferences. My motto is "do what works for you."

Fresh ingredients and whole foods behave differently in recipes every time, so adjust accordingly. Not enough salt? Add some more salt. Not thin enough? Add some liquid. Needs more time in the oven? Cool, let it bake longer. Get in tune with your inner kitchen spirit and listen to what the food is telling you. Yeah, it just got spiritual.

Eat as much as you want. I don't believe in counting calories or restricting the good stuff in life, so these recipes should be eaten in abundance. All the ingredients in this book are what your body wants, so dig in, my hungry bud.

To see more information about ingredients, go to page 179.

TOOLS

You're gonna need a blender, an oven and this thing called a mandolin slicer, but that's pretty much it. I am unbelievably lazy so I tend to use as little equipment as possible.

For blenders I recommend either Vitamix or Blendtec—they both kick ass.

If you have a dehydrator, that's rad, but I personally use my oven at its lowest temperature to dehydrate food for my raw recipes (although I give instructions for both in my recipes). If you do wanna buy a dehydrator, Excalibur is the best one… plus the name is so epic.

And finally, a mandolin slicer is a neat little gadget that slices stuff REALLY thin. I love it for making zucchini noodles or just for decorative salad ingredients; candy cane beets sliced on a mandolin are too pretty. It's fun to use and easy to clean. Alternatively, just slice stuff really thin by hand (good luck though) or use a vegetable spiral slicer or a vegetable peeler.

TECHNIQUES

Blending, baking and slicing: that's what we're gonna be doin'. Oh, and some soaking.

To blend stuff, all you need is a functional hand (or two) to press the right buttons and flip the right switches.

Baking is also fairly straightforward: preheat the oven and away we go. Just make sure you bake food for as long as it needs. When you're working with whole foods, they behave differently every time, so some days a delicata squash will take 30 minutes and other days it'll take 40. Use the senses Momma Nature and evolution bestowed upon you and check periodically when the grub is starting to look and smell done—poke it with a fork to feel the texture and tear off a chunk to taste. Same story for the dehydrator—the only difference is that it's set at gentler temperatures.

As far as slicing goes: just don't be stupid. Pay attention when you are cutting food with sharp objects like a mandolin slicer or knives and save the kitchen dance party for when the blades are washed and put away (but definitely HAVE the kitchen dance party after that). Mandolin slicers come with a safety guard to hold whatever you're cutting in place and so that your fingers don't have to be directly near the blade. Always use the safety guard, 'mkay?

In a few recipes I list soaked nuts as an ingredient, so here's how you soak nuts: rinse the nuts (use raw, unsalted and preferably organic), put 'em in a big bowl and cover with cold water by at least a couple inches, add around ½ teaspoon of salt and leave the nuts to soak for as long as suggested in the recipe you're looking at. The harder the nuts, the longer they will need to soak. Then drain and rinse them thoroughly and they're good to go.

RAW

Why eat raw food? Because it's fun, delicious and really good for you. Although some foods are actually more nutritious when they are lightly cooked, there are also many that are healthier when left raw (like bell peppers). This is why I eat both raw and cooked food. It's not about sticking to diet labels; it's about living in a way that makes you feel healthy and happy. I personally feel best eating a mostly raw diet, but everyone is different so find out what works for you and do that. I like these recipes when I want a lighter meal or when I want to feel more energetic in the evening.

Raw foods can be anything from salads, smoothies and juices to sauces, soups and surprisingly delectable main meals (as you will soon see). When you leave your ingredients raw, you can potentially leave in a lot of flavor and nutrition, but my favorite thing about raw food recipes is the colors. A carefully sliced heirloom tomato served with a little black pepper and salt is a sexy piece of art that tastes like fresh pizza. The recipes in this chapter are all pretty quick to make; they are hydrating, nutrient-dense, colorful and taste great.

Get the glow, eat raw.

> NOTE: For all intents and purposes, every recipe in this chapter serves 2 to 3.

PSYCHEDELIC SALAD

Shredded Carrots, Red Cabbage + Beets with Lemon Sesame Dressing

I couldn't stop staring at this after I arranged it on the plate. Looking at the bright stripes in a candy cane beet kiiiinda makes me consider Creationism, but no. Evolution is way cooler. This is a really fresh mix of juicy, crunchy veggies paired with a tangy, creamy sauce that's excellent for refreshing your palate anytime ya need to.

SALAD

1 small candy cane beet

1 small yellow beet

1 large carrot

1 small red cabbage

3 cups (171 g) leafy greens

LEMON SESAME DRESSING

½ cup (118 ml) water

¼ cup (56 g) tahini

2 tbsp (30 ml) fresh lemon juice

½ tsp sea salt

GARNISH

½ avocado

1 tsp black sesame seeds

1 tsp extra virgin olive oil (optional)

To make the salad: peel the beets and carrot and remove the outer leaves of the cabbage. Shred the yellow beet, carrot and cabbage on a mandolin slicer or by hand. Slice the candy cane beet widthwise very thinly, on a mandolin slicer or by hand. Set everything aside while you make the dressing.

To make the dressing: blend all the ingredients together until smooth.

Toss the greens in this dressing, then arrange on a plate or in a bowl. Top with the avocado, shredded veggies and candy cane beet, then garnish by sprinkling on sesame seeds and drizzling some olive oil.

ZUCCHINI NOODLES

with Garlic Kale Pesto + Hemp Seeds

Soooooo sensuous. I think kale is sexy, and when you smother it all over some fresh raw zucchini along with garlic and hemp seeds… ah, it's heaven. Get your healthy fats right here, folks.

ZUCCHINI NOODLES

2 medium zucchinis

GARLIC KALE PESTO

2 peeled garlic cloves

¼ cup (31 g) pine nuts

¼ tsp sea salt

¼ tsp black pepper

¾ cup (50 g) fresh kale

¼ cup (10 g) fresh basil

¼ cup (59 ml) extra virgin olive oil

GARNISH

2 tbsp (19 g) hulled hemp seeds

To make the noodles: slice the zucchinis—on a mandolin slicer, spiral slicer or cheese grater—into thin noodles. Place all the noodles on a towel and let them sit for 30 minutes so they dry out a little.

To make the pesto: throw all the ingredients into a food processor and process until you get your desired consistency. Massage the pesto into your noodles by hand or with a wooden spoon and let this sit a few minutes more to soften and let the noodles soak up some flavor. Sprinkle with hemp seeds and enjoy.

RAINBOW WRAPS

This recipe couldn't be any easier. It's full of whole foods, vibrant colors and delicious flavors. I love eating this with tahini. Personally I find that the lemon juice adds a tangy punch so I don't need salt, but add a sprinkle if you want. And FYI: you can use whatever veggies you like! Tomato, onion, baked yam, steamed spinach, pepper, cucumber; whatever floats your boat (or in this case, fills up your wrap).

FILLINGS

1 small beet

1 small zucchini

1 medium carrot

1 avocado

2 tbsp (30 ml) fresh lemon juice

WRAPS

2 nori sheets

¼ cup (56 g) tahini (optional)

Slice the beet, zucchini and carrot on a mandolin slicer, spiral slicer or cheese grater, into thin strips. Cut open the avocado and spoon out the meat into a bowl with the lemon juice, mashing it up with a fork.

Spread the avocado-lemon mixture onto the nori sheets, add the strips of pre-cut veggies, roll it up and slice the wraps in half. Enjoy with some tahini if you want.

CREAMY MISO SOUP

with Baby Shiitake Mushrooms + Sea Vegetables

I basically inhaled this recipe, so it's a miracle I was able to snap some photos of the bowl before it was empty. Try to find organic, locally grown mushrooms (I get mine from the farmer's market) because their texture and flavor makes all the difference. The kelp and dulse (greens from the sea) add a natural saltiness and deep notes to the earthiness of the 'shrooms.

MARINATED MUSHROOMS

2 cups (118 g) baby shiitake mushrooms

1 tsp extra virgin olive oil

1 tsp gluten-free tamari

1 tsp fresh lemon juice

CREAMY MISO SOUP

¼ cup (31 g) pine nuts

2 tbsp (20 g) hulled hemp seeds

2 tbsp (20 g) white sesame seeds

2 tbsp (28 g) miso paste

½ tsp dried dill

½ tsp ginger powder

½ tsp kelp granules

2 cups (473 ml) hot water

GARNISH

2 sprigs fresh parsley

½ tsp dulse flakes

1 tsp white sesame seeds

To prepare the mushrooms: slice them thinly then toss with the olive oil, tamari and lemon juice. Let them sit somewhere warm for 30 minutes so they can marinate.

To make the soup base: blend all the ingredients until smooth. If you want it super smooth, strain through a cheesecloth or a nut milk bag.

Scoop the mushrooms evenly into 2 bowls, then pour the soup over them and garnish with parsley, dulse flakes and sesame seeds.

KOHLRABI + BEET SALAD

with Green Tahini Sauce

Kohlrabi is a popular snack in the Middle East, where it's simply sliced thinly, drizzled in olive oil and sprinkled with salt. In this recipe, I'm adding some other flavors and colors like beets and fresh herbs to take this healthy root to the next level.

SALAD

1 small kohlrabi

1 small red beet

1 tsp extra virgin olive oil

1 tsp fresh lemon juice

GREEN TAHINI SAUCE

⅓ cup (79 ml) water

1 tbsp (14 g) tahini

½ cup (20 g) fresh cilantro

½ cup (20 g) fresh parsley

½ tsp sea salt (optional)

1 peeled garlic clove

1 tsp chunk poolod gingor

GARNISH

1 tsp white sesame seeds

To prepare the salad: peel the kohlrabi and beet, slice very thinly on a mandolin slicer or by hand, then toss with the olive oil and lemon juice.

To make the sauce: blend everything until smooth. If you'd like it less watery, add 1 tablespoon (14 g) more of tahini, or even ½ cup (120 g) cooked chickpeas if you want a hummus-like dip.

Arrange your kohlrabi and beet slices however you like, and serve beside the sauce. I sprinkled some sesame seeds on mine because I sprinkle them on basically everything.

EPIC PORTABELLO YAM BURGERS

with Parsley, Herb Cheeze + Shredded Veg

The name says it all.

BUNS

2 tsp (10 ml) extra virgin olive oil

2 tsp (10 ml) gluten-free tamari

4 portabello mushroom caps

BURGERS

1 medium yam

1 cup (50 g) chopped green onion

1 tbsp (14 g) miso paste

1 tsp cumin powder

1 tsp paprika powder

½ tsp dried rosemary

½ tsp dried savory

½ tsp chili powder

½ cup (76 g) hulled hemp seeds

HERB CHEEZE

½ cup (76 g) Brazil nuts

1 tbsp (15 ml) fresh lemon juice

½ tsp sea salt, as desired

1 tsp dried rosemary

1 tsp dried basil

ADD-ONS

¼ cup (25 g) shredded carrot

¼ cup (25 g) shredded beet

½ cup (20 g) fresh parsley

2 tsp (7 g) white sesame seeds

To make the buns: rub the olive oil and tamari into the mushroom caps, then marinate in a dehydrator at 115°F (46°C) for 2 hours, or until they have darkened and are soft and juicy. Alternatively, use your oven at its lowest temperature until you get the same result, around 1 hour.

To make the burgers: wash and peel the yam, then chop into ½-inch (13-mm) pieces. Throw the chopped yam along with the rest of the ingredients in your food processor and process until it becomes a mushy paste (albeit really yummy). Form into ¼ cup (53 g) patties using a cookie mold or your hands. Dehydrate at 115°F (46°C) in the dehydrator for 1 hour, flip them over, then bake for 1 more hour or until they can hold their shape when you pick them up. Alternatively, use your oven at its lowest temperature 'til you get the same result, about 1 hour.

To make the cheeze: blend all the ingredients together until smooth and delicious!

Layer up on a portabello cap: the shredded veg, parsley, a patty, some cheeze and more shredded beets and carrots. Top it off with another mushroom cap and sprinkle with sesame seeds. Repeat with the other patty. EPIC.

SWEET CORN CHOWDER

with Garlic, Miso + Walnuts

This soup was inspired by one in Ani Phyo's *Raw Food Kitchen*, which was the first raw vegan cookbook I bought when I was 16 years old. Her sweet corn chowder and mushroom soup recipes quickly became favorites of mine and helped me learn how to experiment with creating my own dishes. This soup is filling, very nutritious and comes together in just a few minutes. Make sure to find organic, non-GMO corn.

2 ½ cups (379 g) sweet corn kernels, soaked for 10 minutes in hot water then rinsed

2 cups (473 ml) hot water

4 peeled garlic cloves

1 tbsp (14 g) chunk peeled ginger

1 tsp mustard

1 tbsp (14 g) miso paste

¼ cup (30 g) walnuts, soaked for 4 hours

Blend all the ingredients, except for a ½ cup (76 g) of corn (which you'll add later), in a high-speed blender until smooth. Adjust according to taste, adding salt, pepper or other seasonings if desired.

Pour into bowls and top off with the rest of the corn.

NORI WRAPS

with Marinated Enoki Mushrooms, Purple Cabbage + Greens

Enoki mushrooms are too cute. You can use rice paper wraps if you don't like nori, and if you wanna take this to the next level, use the Tangy Tahini Dressing (page 63) as a dipping sauce.

MARINATED MUSHROOMS

3 cups (177 g) enoki mushrooms

1 tbsp (15 ml) apple cider vinegar

1 tbsp (15 ml) gluten-free tamari

1 tsp agave syrup

1 tsp paprika powder

½ tsp cumin powder

⅛ tsp chili powder

2 tsp (9 g) tahini

WRAPS

4 nori sheets

2 cups (681 g) shredded collard greens

1 cup (55 g) shredded butter lettuce

1 cup (341 g) shredded purple cabbage

1 cup (119 q) cucumber, sliced into strips

¾ cup (30 g) cilantro leaves

Toss the mushrooms with the rest of the ingredients and dehydrate for 2 hours at 115°F (46°C), or until they have softened and start to smell aromatic. Alternatively, you can use your oven at its lowest temperature until you get the same result, around 1 hour.

To make the wraps: put a little bit of everything into the nori sheets and wrap it up!

MANGO + COCONUT SALAD

with Fresh Basil

My partner's aunt made something similar to this when we visited her and her partner one night. I couldn't get the flavors of fresh, juicy mango and creamy, cooling coconut outta my head for several days afterwards, so I had to make my own version. It's so freaking yummy.

4 large mangoes, slightly pre-ripe

2 cups (160 g) young coconut meat

¼ cup (10 g) fresh basil

1 tsp fresh lime juice, or more as desired

Peel the mangoes then slice them into thin strips on a mandolin slicer or by hand. Slice the coconut meat into thin strips by hand.

If you want to make a dressing to go with the salad, simply blend 3 tablespoons (15 g) of the coconut meat and 3 tablespoons (15 g) of the mango with 3 tablespoons (44 ml) of water (or coconut water)!

Toss the mango, coconut and basil together and add the dressing if desired, spritz on some lime juice and enjoy!

YAMMY SOUP

with Ginger, Fennel + Coconut Milk

Mmm! This tastes incredible and, as long as you blend it long enough, it comes out ultra-smooth as well. I think the coconut milk drizzled on top adds an elegant touch. For a more filling meal, pair this with avocado toast (just spread some avocado on toast... best snack ever) or any salad in this book.

1 medium yam

1 cup (80 g) young coconut meat

2 cups (473 ml) hot water

½ red bell pepper

1 tsp turmeric powder

1 tbsp (14 g) chunk peeled ginger

½ tsp dried fennel seeds

2 tbsp (28 g) miso paste

Peel the yam. Blend the coconut meat with the water to make coconut milk. Scoop 2 to 3 tablespoons (30 to 44 ml) out of the coconut milk and set aside (this will be drizzled on top in a moment). Blend everything else together until smooth. If your blender has a "soup" function, use it. Otherwise, blend until it's very smooth just like cooked soup. It may take a minute or two, and you can give your blender breaks if needed.

Adjust according to taste, adding more miso or spices if you want. Pour into bowls and drizzle with the remaining coconut milk. Enjoy!

SUSHI: MAKI ROLLS

with Avocado, Carrot, Bell Pepper + Cauliflower Rice

Rice-free sushi? Huh? Yeah, baby. We are using cauliflower instead. Oh and by the way, when "sushi" is rolled like this, it's actually called maki. Personally I love cooked rice, and I think it is part of a healthy diet, but there are days when I want a lighter meal, and that is where raw dishes come in. This would be fantastic with any sauces I have featured in other recipes, but peanut sauce is my fave for maki rolls.

CAULIFLOWER RICE

1 small head cauliflower

1 tsp dried dill

1 tsp rice vinegar

⅛ tsp stevia powder

FILLINGS

1 avocado

½ bell pepper

1 large carrot

4 nori sheets

Peanut Lime Sauce (page 129)

To make the rice: process the cauliflower in a food processor until it becomes a bunch of little crumbs. In a bowl, stir in the rest of the ingredients by hand with the cauliflower.

Julienne all the vegetables (in other words, cut into thin strips).

For each nori sheet, spread on ¼ of the rice evenly, leaving one edge of about ½-inch (1-cm) without rice. Sprinkle a little water on this edge when you roll up the sheet, starting from the opposite side. This will help everything stick together. Arrange a few slices of avocado, pepper and carrot. Roll up tightly and cut with a sharp knife. Serve with the peanut sauce.

GARDEN BURRITOS

with Spicy Mushroom Nut Meat, Guacamole + Broccolini

Filling, flavorful, fantastic. These would be great with whole grain, gluten-free wraps or corn tortillas as well. And as usual: drizzling tahini is highly recommended.

SPICY MUSHROOM NUT MEAT

1 cup (170 g) almonds, soaked for 8 hours

1 ½ cups (71 g) mushrooms

½ tsp cumin powder

½ tsp coriander powder

¼ tsp chili flakes

¼ tsp sea salt

¼ tsp black pepper

GUACAMOLE

2 avocados

2 tbsp (30 ml) fresh lime juice

½ tsp sea salt

FILLINGS

3 cups (689 g) broccolini

1 tbsp (8 g) gluten-free tamari

4 huge collard leaves

1 cup (40 g) cilantro

1 cup (341 g) shredded purple cabbage

To make the nut meat: put all the ingredients in a food processor and process until it forms a chunky paste. Adjust according to taste, adding more spice or salt if desired.

To make the guacamole: mash the avocado meat with the lime juice and salt until it reaches the desired consistency (I like mine a little chunky).

Toss the broccolini with the tamari and let sit in the oven at 200°F (93°C) for 10 to 15 minutes to soften, or use a dehydrator at 115°F (46°C) for 40 minutes. If your oven doesn't go that low, just use the lowest temperature and keep an eye on the food since you may need to take it out a few minutes early.

Spread your mushroom nut meat onto the collard leaves, and add in the guac, cilantro, cabbage and broccolini. Wrap up and enjoy!

ZUCCHINI NOODLES

with Lime Juice, Tahini, Parsley + Green Onions

I love adding lemon and lime juice to recipes—it bumps up the flavor and nutrition at the same time. This recipe is light, tangy, creamy and very hydrating. Eat ASAP because zucchini flesh starts letting out its juices quickly after you cut it.

4 zucchinis

¼ cup (59 ml) fresh lime juice

¼ cup (56 g) tahini

2 tbsp (20 g) white sesame seeds

1 cup (40 g) fresh parsley leaves

¼ cup (12 g) chopped green onions

1 tsp Himalayan salt

Wash all the produce. Slice the zucchinis into noodles on a mandolin slicer or by hand. Toss the noodles with the rest of the ingredients and eat!

SUMMER ROLLS

with Shredded Veg, Avocado, Basil, Mint + Dipping Sauce

Crunchy, light, fresh and flavorful. I could eat these all year long. Well, I kinda do that already.

FILLINGS

2 large carrots

1 cup (341 g) purple cabbage

1 avocado

1 cup (40 g) lightly packed basil leaves

1 cup (40 g) lightly packed mint leaves

WRAPS

6 rice papers (or large collard leaves)

DIPPING SAUCE

3 tbsp (44 ml) water

2 tbsp (30 ml) fresh lime juice

2 tbsp (5 g) mint leaves

2 tbsp (5 g) basil leaves

1 tbsp (14 g) miso paste

1 tbsp (11 g) almond butter

Chili powder, to taste (optional)

1 tbsp (15 g) white sesame seeds (optional)

Shred the carrots and cabbage. Slice the avocado meat into strips.

Fill a large bowl with warm water. To soften the rice papers, simply dip them (one at a time) into the water for around 10 seconds. Then use like a tortilla: assemble the veggies and herbs on it and wrap up.

To make the dipping sauce: blend all ingredients until smooth. Sprinkle with sesame seeds. Enjoy!

RAWSOME PIZZA

Veggie Crust with Avocado, Tomato, Spinach, Basil + Onion

OMG.

CRUST

½ onion

2 cups (303 g) sweet corn kernels

1 zucchini

¼ cup (40 g) white sesame seeds

¼ cup (40 g) ground flax seeds

2 peeled garlic cloves

½ tsp black pepper

¼ tsp chili powder

¼ tsp cumin powder

1 tsp dried basil

1 tsp dried rosemary

1 tsp dried oregano

1 tbsp (14 g) miso paste

SAUCE

½ cup (83 g) dehydrated tomato slices

½ cup (38 g) chopped zucchini

1 tbsp (15 ml) fresh lemon juice

Handful fresh basil leaves

1 date

1 garlic clove

TOPPINGS

¼ cup (10 g) basil leaves

1 cup (225 g) spinach leaves

1 diced avocado

1 diced tomato

3 tbsp (42 g) tahini

¼ onion, diced

¼ tsp black pepper

½ tsp garlic powder

2 tsp (10 ml) fresh lemon juice

Whatever else you like (Brazil Nut Cheeze on page 80, hint hint)

To make the crust: put everything in your food processor and process until it becomes a paste. Add more spices if you like, but keep in mind the flavor will become intensified after "baking." Add a little olive oil and Himalayan salt if you like. Spread the paste onto a lined baking pan, forming it into a pizza crust shape, but leave it quite thick, around a ⅓-inch (a little less than 1-cm)… it will shrink a lot. Put in the dehydrator at 115°F (46°C) degrees for 7 to 9 hours, or until it is firm all the way through. Alternatively, use the oven at its lowest temperature until you get the same result, around 5 hours. Flip it gently at this point—be careful, it's fragile!—and "bake" for 1 more hour or so until the whole thing is crispy and holds its shape. Let the crust sit out for 1 to 2 hours to cool down.

To make the sauce: put all the ingredients in a food processor or blender and blend until smooth. Spread the sauce on your crust (don't use too much though 'cause it'll make the crust soggy). Decorate with whatever toppings you like and awaaaaay we go! Best to eat right away.

CARROT DAIKON SALAD

with Lemon Juice + Basil

Daikon is a radish that's big in Asian cooking. I like the bite it has when eaten raw, and it's terrific for cleansing your body. I pair it with carrot here to balance out the bitter with sweet, but I bet mango would be an amazing addition or substitute.

2 large carrots

1 medium daikon

2 tbsp (30 ml) fresh lemon juice

1 tsp maple syrup

¼ tsp sea salt

¼ tsp chili flakes (optional)

½ cup (20 g) tightly packed fresh basil

1 tbsp (15 g) pumpkin seeds

Wash and peel the carrots and daikon. Shred into strips.

Stir together the lemon juice, maple syrup, salt and chili (if using). Toss with the shredded veg. Slice the basil leaves into thin strips and add to the rest. Top with pumpkin seeds and nom it down.

ARUGULA LEAVES

with Golden Beet, Kiwi, Radish + Orange Juice Dressing

Arugula has a very special flavor; some like it and some don't. It is slightly nutty with a kind of radish-y aftertaste. I think the sweet fruits in this recipe help to balance it out, and this recipe might be amazing with some Almond Thyme Pâté (page 79).

SALAD

2 kiwis

1 large golden beet

5 radishes

1 peeled orange

2 tbsp (17 g) chia seeds

8 cups (322 g) arugula leaves

DRESSING

4 tbsp (59 ml) fresh orange juice

2 tbsp (28 g) tahini

¼ tsp sea salt

¼ tsp black pepper (optional)

Slice the kiwis, beet and radishes thinly on a mandolin slicer, or shred them if you prefer. Slice the orange into segments. Toss the sliced produce with the chia seeds and arugula.

To make the dressing: blend the orange juice with the other ingredients. Drizzle on the salad and enjoy!

GARLIC-MARINATED MOREL MUSHROOMS

with Heirloom Tomato, Basil Sauce, Radish + Dill

I found morels at the first farmer's market of the summer this year and knew I had to try them out in a raw recipe for this book. If you cannot find morels, substitute in shiitakes or any other 'shroom you like.

MUSHROOMS

2 cups (118 g) morel mushrooms

¼ cup (59 ml) extra virgin olive oil, as needed

2 peeled garlic cloves

BASIL SAUCE

⅓ cup (13 g) fresh basil leaves

1 tbsp (14 g) tahini

1 tbsp (14 g) miso paste

2 tbsp (19 g) chopped onion

¼ cup (59 ml), water, as needed

1 heirloom tomato

2 radishes

1 to 2 tbsp (3 to 6 g) fresh dill, as desired

To marinate the mushrooms: wash them gently and thoroughly, and cut off the white stems. Blend the oil with the garlic and coat the mushrooms in this marinade by hand or with a brush (you will probably have oil left over). Marinate the mushrooms in a dehydrator for around 2 hours at 115°F (46°C)—or in your oven at its lowest temperature, for around 1 hour—until they smell fragrant and have a cooked texture (bite one to find out). Check on them every 20 minutes or so and if they seem dry, add a little more oil.

To make the basil sauce: blend everything together until smooth, adding water in small amounts until you get the consistency you like.

Slice the tomato horizontally, and slice the radishes thinly with a mandolin slicer or by hand. Cut up the mushrooms and throw everything together in a bowl! Alternatively, make it look fancy by spooning drops of the sauce all over a plate, layer with the radishes and decorated with the tomato and 'shroomers. Garnish with dill, if you'd like.

RADISH GREENS

with Cilantro, Lemon, Snap Peas + Avocado

You might think radish greens would be really spicy and bitter, but actually their flavor is quite lovely and mild. Regardless, anything tastes great with some lemon juice, avocado and salt.

1 lemon

7 cups (252 g) radish greens

1 avocado

2 cups (99 g) snap peas

1 cup (40 g) cilantro

1 tsp charcoal salt (or sea salt)

Squeeze the lemon juice onto the greens and set aside. Slice the avocado thinly, and cut the snap peas into halves. Toss everything together, along with the cilantro, mashing the avocado into the greens and veggies. Sprinkle with some salt and eat it all up.

KING OYSTER MUSHROOMS

Layered with Heirloom Tomato, Basil + Avocado

King oyster mushrooms have a unique, chewy texture that reminds me, weirdly enough, of calamari.

LAYERS

3 king oyster mushrooms

1 tbsp (15 ml) gluten-free tamari

2 large heirloom tomatoes

1 avocado

2 sprigs of fresh basil

BASIL OIL

1 cup (237 ml) extra virgin olive oil

½ cup (20 g) fresh basil leaves

To prepare the mushrooms: dice them, then toss with the tamari and leave in the oven at its lowest temperature—or your dehydrator at 115°F (46°C)—for 1 hour, or until the mushrooms have softened and darkened slightly.

Slice the tomatoes and avocado into thin slices. Using the inside of a large circular cookie cutter, layer the mushrooms with the avocado and tomato and top with the basil leaves.

To make the basil oil: blend the oil with the basil. Decorate your plate with this. You'll have lots of basil oil left over so try to use it up within 4 or 5 days. I recommend using it on salads with some balsamic vinegar or grilling fresh vegetables brushed with it for epic summer BBQs.

SWEET CORN QUICHE

with Buckwheat Onion Crust + Cherry Tomatoes

YUSSSSSS.

BUCKWHEAT ONION CRUST

½ cup (85 g) buckwheat groats

½ cup (76 g) roughly chopped onion

¼ cup (23 g) ground flax seed

FILLING

2 cups (303 g) sweet corn

¼ cup (38 g) roughly chopped onion

¼ tsp salt

¼ tsp black pepper

1 tsp dried basil

TOPPING

4 cherry tomatoes

To make the crust: soak the buckwheat groats for 30 minutes in water, then rinse well. Put the groats into a food processor or blender with the onion and flax seed and blend into a thick paste. If it's too dry, add 1 tablespoon (15 ml) of water. If it's too wet or thin, add 1 tablespoon (6 g) of flax seed. Shape into crusts in tart tins and dehydrate for 3 hours at 115°F (46°C), or "bake" at your oven's lowest temperature for about 90 minutes, until the paste has hardened and darkened into a crust.

To make the filling: buzz all the ingredients into a paste in a food processor or blender, and then fill your crusts with this mixture. Top with sliced tomatoes.

Alternatively, you can dehydrate the tomatoes at 115°F (46°C) for 1 hour—or throw 'em in the oven at the lowest temperature available—if you want them to develop more flavor, or just use as is.

KALE SALAD

with Carrot, Pineapple + Coconut Sauce

The sauce in this recipe was an improvised experiment—although let's be real, all my recipes are—that turned out über delicious. That's why it's in here. Plus, the color: hello!?

CARROT, PINEAPPLE + COCONUT SAUCE

1 large carrot

½ cup (40 g) young coconut meat

½ cup (118 ml) pineapple juice

⅛ tsp sea salt

⅛ tsp chili flakes (optional)

SALAD

8 cups (340 g) baby kale leaves

1 cup (40 g) fresh parsley

1 cup (161 g) halved cherry tomatoes

2 tbsp (20 g) pumpkin seeds

2 tbsp (15 g) chopped walnuts

Peel the carrot then slice it thinly on a mandolin slicer. Throw half the carrot slices into a blender and blend with the coconut meat and pineapple juice until smooth. If it's too thick, add more pineapple juice or some lemon juice. Add the salt and chili flakes to the sauce, tasting as you go. Toss the carrots, kale and parsley in the sauce along with everything else. Woo!

PHO BOWL

with Basil, Mint, Chives, Bok Choy + Leeks

I love the aromatic broth in this recipe; I could drink it all by itself. When you're craving greens, this bowl will satisfy.

BROTH

5 peeled garlic cloves

3 tbsp (43 g) chunk peeled ginger

⅓ cup (51 g) roughly chopped onion

3 cloves

1 tsp cinnamon powder

1 ½ tsp (4 g) coriander powder

3 cardamom pods

4 cups (946 ml) hot vegetable broth

1 to 2 tsp (5 to 10 ml) gluten-free tamari (optional)

VEG

2 zucchinis

2 cups (140 g) baby bok choy

¼ cup (12 g) finely chopped chives

¼ cup (38 g) finely chopped leeks

½ cup (20 g) fresh basil leaves

½ cup (20 g) fresh mint leaves

To make the broth: blend everything together until smooth. Taste and adjust accordingly, adding more spices or some tamari if you'd like.

Slice the zucchini into noodles on a mandolin slicer or by hand. Place the bok choy in a bowl of steaming water for a few minutes so it softens.

Throw all the veg and herbs into a bowl, then pour the broth over everything and enjoy! If you want it to taste a little heartier, go ahead and simmer this in a pot before eating; it'll soften the bok choy and noodles.

SOM TAM

Green Papaya Salad

My parents volunteered in Thailand for a couple of years before they decided to move to British Columbia and start a family. *Som tam* is a popular and spicy salad in Thailand, usually eaten with sticky rice. Fortunately, we have a terrific Thai restaurant a few minutes away from our house and the chefs grew up in the same region my parents lived in; they make a mean *som tam*. This is my version, and I definitely recommend you eat it with sticky rice and/or mango.

¼ cup (38 g) jungle peanuts

½ cup (80 g) cherry tomatoes

½ cup (50 g) green beans

3 cups (165 g) green papaya

¼ cup (59 ml) fresh lemon juice, or more as desired

⅛ tsp chili pepper flakes

1 tsp agave syrup

¼ cup (10 g) roughly chopped basil leaves

Crush the peanuts in a mortar and pestle (or with a knife) and set aside. Slice the tomatoes into quarters. Slice the green beans into 1-inch (2.5-cm)-long pieces. Shred the papaya on a mandolin slicer or by hand.

In the mortar and pestle, add all the ingredients together, except the peanuts, and mash gently so it all combines into a salad. Use a wooden spoon to get everything evenly coated. If you don't have a mortar and pestle, just throw everything together in a bowl with salad spoons. Adjust according to taste, adding whatever else you like. Sprinkle with the peanuts and enjoy!

> NOTE: If you cannot find green papaya, use rutabaga instead.

GET YOUR GREENZ

Leafy Salad with Green Onions, Zucchini Strips, Purple Cabbage + Tangy Tahini Dressing

This was an impromptu recipe like so many others that I made up on the spot, but I loved it so much I decided to write it down here.

SALAD

2 zucchinis

2 cups (110 g) butter lettuce

2 cups (72 g) collard greens

1 cup (40 g) fresh cilantro

1 cup (40 g) fresh parsley

2 tbsp (10 g) pumpkin seeds

¼ cup (84 g) shredded purple cabbage

¼ cup (12 g) sliced green onion

TANGY TAHINI DRESSING

2 tbsp (30 ml) apple cider vinegar

2 tbsp (28 g) tahini

1 tbsp (14 g) miso paste

2 tbsp (30 ml) water

Slice the zucchinis into thin strips on a mandolin slicer or by hand. Chop up the greens and then throw all the salad ingredients together.

To make the dressing: blend everything until smooth then drizzle onto your salad. Yum. Add more tahini or salt right onto the salad if you like.

RAW TACOS

with Sweet Corn, Kiwi, Cumin-Marinated Tomatoes + Pea Shoots

Holy SMOKES these are good.

3 cups (483 g) baby tomatoes

2 tsp (5 g) cumin powder

4 kiwis

1 head butter lettuce

2 cups (303 g) sweet corn kernels

½ cup (20 g) pea shoots

1 sliced avocado (optional)

Cut up the tomatoes and put 'em in a dehydrator for 1 to 2 hours at 115°F (46°C) until they get juicy and their skin gets slightly wrinkly. You can also use your oven at its lowest temperature until the same thing happens—it'll take around 40 minutes.

Toss the juicy tomatoes with the cumin. Peel and slice up the kiwis. Rinse the lettuce gently and separate the leaves.

Fill each lettuce leaf with tomatoes, kiwi, corn, pea shoots and avocado, then wrap up and eaaaaat.

SHAVED FENNEL

with Grapefruit, Avocado + Radishes

Fennel tastes subtly similar to licorice, although botanically they're not related. The plant kingdom is too cool. I like to mash up the avocado with the rest of the salad so you get this thick, creamy kind of dressing.

1 radish

1 fennel bulb

1 avocado, sliced thinly

¼ cup (10 g) pea shoots

1 large grapefruit, cut into sections

2 tbsp (30 ml) fresh lemon juice

¼ tsp sea salt

¼ tsp black pepper

½ tsp black sesame seeds

On a mandolin slicer or by hand, slice the radish and 1 cup (87 g) of the fennel into thin pieces. Grate the rest of the fennel. Toss all the fennel and radish with the avocado, pea shoots and grapefruit. Sprinkle on lemon juice, salt, pepper and sesame seeds as you like and enjoy!

STUFFED TOMATOES

with Carrot-Cauliflower Filling

Cute little guys, aren't they?

CARROT-CAULIFLOWER FILLING

1 cup (230 g) chopped cauliflower

1 cup (151 g) chopped carrots

1 ½ tsp (7 ml) fresh lemon juice

1 tsp gluten-free tamari

1 tsp maple syrup

¼ cup (40 g) hemp seeds

¼ cup (10 g) roughly chopped cilantro leaves

3 tbsp (9 g) fresh dill

½ tsp sea salt

¼ tsp black pepper

6 medium tomatoes

To make the filling: throw the cauliflower in a food processor and process for just a few seconds until it becomes a grainy mixture. Put into a large bowl and set aside. Do the same for the carrot and add to the same bowl. Now toss this mixture with the rest of the ingredients. Taste and adjust accordingly, adding some salt, more maple syrup, some herbs or spices—whatever you like.

Cut off the tops of the tomatoes and scoop out the insides. You can add the insides to the filling if you like. Fill each tomato with the carrot-cauliflower mix and enjoy!

RADICCHIO SALAD

with Parsley, Sunflower Seeds, Carrot + Spirulina Dressing

Mmm. My partner, Jack and I were goin' at this bowl like it was the last salad on earth. I literally was grabbing pieces of cabbage with my hands. Note to self (and everyone else): wash your face after eating this one.

SALAD

2 heads radicchio cabbage

2 large carrots

2 cups (80 g) fresh parsley

SPIRULINA DRESSING

¼ cup (56 g) tahini

1 tsp spirulina, as needed

2 to 4 tbsp (30 to 59 ml) water, as needed

3 tbsp (45 ml) fresh lemon juice

½ tsp sea salt

1 tsp garlic powder

2 tbsp (20 g) black sesame seeds (optional)

¼ cup (34 g) sunflower seeds

To make the salad: peel the first layer of leaves off the cabbage and discard. Peel the carrots. Wash all the veg. Rip the cabbage up into bite size pieces and shred the carrots. Throw all the veg in a big bowl.

To make the dressing: blend everything until smooth, adding water and spirulina as needed to get the consistency, flavor and color you prefer. Adjust according to taste, adding more salt, garlic, whatever you like.

Pour onto the veg and mix up a little. Top with the seeds and chow down.

LETTUCE, SORREL,

Pea Greens, Fava Greens, Tomatoes, Shredded Veg + Thick Parsley Dressing

As long as you dig parsley, you'll love this one.

SALAD

1 cup (40 g) pea greens

1 cup (40 g) fava bean greens

1 cup (40 g) sorrel

1 head lettuce

1 carrot

1 red beet

6 baby Roma tomatoes

¼ cup (12 g) green onion

2 baby cucumbers

PARSLEY DRESSING

1 cup (40 g) fresh parsley

¼ cup (29 g) pumpkin seeds

¼ cup (59 ml) fresh lemon juice

½ cup (118 ml) water

½ tsp sea salt

¼ tsp black pepper

½ tsp coconut sugar

1 tbsp (14 g) tahini

2 peeled garlic cloves

To prepare the salad: wash all the produce. Tear the greens into bite size pieces, shred the carrot and beet, cut the tomatoes in half and chop the green onion and cucumbers.

To make the dressing: blend everything until smooth. Adjust according to preference; if it's too thick, add more water, if you want it saltier, add more salt! You know the drill.

Toss the greens with the dressing in a bowl and decorate with all the veg on top.

MASSAGED GREEN SALAD

with Creamy Purple Dressing + Cucumber

Nice to look at, nicer to eat.

SALAD

1 big bunch kale

½ avocado

1 peeled white beet

1 cucumber

½ cup (170 g) chopped purple cabbage

½ tsp white sesame seeds

¼ cup (38 g) raisins

Some fresh dill sprigs (optional)

DRESSING

¼ cup (28 g) cashews, soaked for 3 hours

¼ cup (85 g) chopped purple cabbage

1 tbsp (14 g) miso paste

1 tbsp (15 ml) maple syrup

1 tbsp (15 ml) fresh lemon juice

¼ cup (59 ml) water

Rip the kale into bite size pieces. Cut up the avocado meat and massage it into the kale leaves. Cut the beet and cucumber into small bite size pieces and set aside.

To make the dressing: blend everything together until smooth and fairly thick. Scoop onto your kale leaves, mix in evenly and then add the rest of the salad ingredients.

GREEN COCONUT CURRY

with Marinated 'Shrooms, Broccoli + Tomato

Another recipe I could not stop eating. The coconut meat cools down the heat from the curry, and all the different colors and textures add up to one really great bowl of food.

MARINATED VEG

3 cups (199 g) sliced mushrooms

3 cups (689 g) small broccoli florets

1 tsp maple syrup

2 tsp (10 ml) fresh lemon juice

2 tsp (10 ml) gluten-free tamari

2 tsp (10 ml) extra virgin olive oil

CURRY

¾ cup (60 g) young coconut meat

¾ cup (23 g) spinach leaves

1 tsp maple syrup

2 tsp (9 g) green curry paste (or your fave curry powder)

1 cup (237 ml) water (or more, as needed)

TOPPINGS

1 large heirloom tomato, chopped

1 cup (40 g) cilantro leaves

To marinate the veg: toss the 'shrooms and broccoli with the maple syrup, lemon juice, tamari and olive oil. Dehydrate for 1 hour at 115°F (46°C) or leave in your oven at its lowest temperature for 45 to 60 minutes. The veggies are ready when they've softened and shrunk a little.

To make the curry: blend everything until smooth, adding water as needed to get the desired consistency. If you'd like to add some salt or tamari, go ahead.

Fill the bowls with curry, add the marinated veggies, tomato chunks and cilantro. Yes!

BEET RAVIOLI

with Almond Thyme Pâté + Basil

One of my favorite recipes in here for REAL. These are decadent and beautiful, but secretly so easy to make. They're more of an appetizer than a main course, so I'd suggest serving them with a large salad (or whatever else you want—I'm not your boss).

ALMOND THYME PÂTÉ

1 cup (170 g) almonds, soaked for 8 hours

2 tbsp (30 ml) fresh lemon juice

⅛ tsp Himalayan salt

2 peeled garlic cloves

2 to 3 tsp (2 to 3 g) fresh thyme leaves (or more, as desired)

1 peeled beet

3 tbsp (8 g) chopped basil leaves

1 tsp fresh thyme leaves

To make the pâté: blend everything together until smooth and thick. Adjust according to taste, adding more salt or thyme or whatever you desire. Scoop onto a cheesecloth (or parchment paper) and roll up into a cylinder shape. I like to add extra thyme leaves here to coat the outside of the pâté; it just looks pretty. Put in the fridge overnight, or if you REALLY want ravioli, for at least a couple hours.

Slice the beet as thin as possible on a mandolin slicer. Scoop 1 teaspoon or so of the pâté onto half of a beet slice and fold the other half over the pâté. It will hold itself in place. Taste this one and see if you want more or less pâté and assemble the rest of the raviolis accordingly. You should have leftover pâté, unless you want to make a ton of raviolis (by all means, go for it). Sprinkle with basil and thyme and enjoy!

LASAGNA

Zucchini Noodles, Heirloom Tomato, Sweet Corn + Brazil Nut Cheeze

Jack thinks this is one of the best savory recipes I've ever made… and he tries like EVERYTHING I make.

VEG

1 small zucchini

2 cups (303 g) sweet corn

1 tbsp (2 g) Herbes de Provence

1 large heirloom tomato

BRAZIL NUT CHEEZE

½ cup (76 g) Brazil nuts

1 tbsp (14 g) tahini

1 tbsp (15 ml) gluten-free tamari

2 peeled garlic cloves

1 tbsp (14 g) miso paste

¼ cup (59 ml) fresh lemon juice

2 tbsp (30 ml) water

2 sprigs fresh basil

To prepare the veg: slice the zucchini thinly, on a mandolin slicer or by hand, into lasagna noodles! Throw the corn into a blender with the Herbes de Provence for just a second so it gets chopped up into a chunky mixture. Slice the tomato thinly.

To make the cheeze: blend everything together until smooth and thick. If you need to add more water, go ahead.

In a lined baking pan (I use a 5-inch x 3-inch [13 x 7.6-cm] bread pan), layer the zucchini with the tomato, corn and cheeze. Refrigerate for 1 hour, until it sets, then gently lift out of the pan, slice in half, top with basil and enjoy.

QUICK TOMATO SOUP

with Miso + Thyme

SO GOOD. Get your heirloom tomatoes from the farmer's market; they are magic. And if you want the tomato flavor to be stronger, let them sit in the dehydrator at 115°F (46°C) for 1 to 2 hours before blending them with everything else (ooor in your oven at its lowest temperature for 30 to 60 minutes).

SOUP

4 cups (644 g) chopped heirloom tomato

3 to 5 peeled garlic cloves, as desired

2 tbsp (28 g) miso paste

2 tbsp (28 g) tahini

2 tsp (10 ml) maple syrup

½ cup (118 ml) vegetable broth (or water)

¼ cup (45 g) cashew butter (optional)

TOPPINGS

¼ tsp black pepper

2 tsp (2 g) fresh thyme leaves

1 ½ cups (228 g) cooked chickpeas (not raw, but really yummy with the soup), optional

To make the soup: blend everything until smooth, adding garlic as you like and cashew butter if you want it creamier. Adjust according to taste and desired consistency.

Pour into bowls and top with thyme, pepper and chickpeas. Nom.

SPICY NOODLE BOWL

with Beet, Carrot, Zucchini + Sweet Tamarind Sauce

This is inspired by pad thai, but tastes a billion times fresher. Everyone in the house wanted a bite.

SWEET TAMARIND SAUCE

2 tbsp (28 g) tamarind paste

½ cup (118 ml) hot water, as needed

2 tbsp (29 g) chunk peeled ginger

4 peeled garlic cloves

2 tsp (10 ml) maple syrup

2 tsp (10 ml) gluten-free tamari

2 tbsp (28 g) tahini

NOODLES

2 beets

2 zucchinis

2 large carrots

TOPPINGS

1 cup (161 g) chopped baby tomatoes

1 cup (40 g) cilantro leaves

½ tsp white sesame seeds (optional)

½ tsp black sesame seeds (optional)

To make the sauce: blend everything together until smooth, adding water as needed. Adjust the flavor as you like.

To make the noodles: wash, peel and slice all the veg using a mandolin, a vegetable spiral slicer or a vegetable peeler.

Toss the noodles with the sauce and then garnish with the toppings. YUMMAY.

SWEET CORN, BABY TOMATO

+ Chimichurri Mix Up

So my "chimichurri" turned into a lime cilantro thingy, but my original inspiration WAS chimichurri—a parsley, olive oil and garlic marinade—so I'm leavin' it. This would be delicious with traditional chimichurri, I am sure. My version is almost like salsa when you add in the corn and tomatoes. This is a crunchy, juicy, savory and zesty recipe that would be peeeerfect for summer BBQs.

2 ears sweet corn

2 cups (322 g) baby heirloom tomatoes

CHIMICHURRI

1 bunch cilantro

3 peeled garlic cloves

2 tbsp (30 ml) fresh lime juice

1 tbsp (15 ml) maple syrup

1 tsp gluten-free tamari

¼ tsp black pepper

Slice all the kernels off the corn and place in a big bowl. Cut all the tomatoes in half and add to the corn kernels. Set aside.

To make the chimichurri: chop the cilantro as finely as possible and mince the garlic. Mix together the cilantro and garlic in a bowl with the rest of the ingredients. Throw on your tomatoes and corn. Mix it up. Yummay in yo tummay.

TOMATO STACKS

with Avocado, Corn + Spices

When you have gorgeous organic produce to work with, it speaks for itself.

2 heirloom tomatoes

1 avocado

1 cup (151 g) sweet corn kernels

1 tbsp (15 ml) extra virgin olive oil

¼ tsp Himalayan salt

¼ tsp black pepper

½ tsp fresh thyme leaves

Slice the tomatoes and avocado into disks, then stack on top of each other and throw on some corn. Drizzle on olive oil, sprinkle on salt, pepper and thyme. Eat.

FARMER'S MARKET BOUNTY

Mixed Greens with Garlic Shoots, Baby Tomatoes, Green Onions, Golden Beets
+ Lemony Ginger Dressing

Nearly all of these ingredients came from the weekly farmer's market, which makes them sooooo delicious, probably
more nutritious and definitely best for the planet. Farmer's markets are often cheaper than the grocery store and the
quality is incomparable. Buy organic, buy local!

SALAD

1 cup (161 g) sliced baby tomatoes

2 medium golden beets

5 cups (100 g) mixed greens

¼ cup (12 g) chopped green onions

½ cup (25 g) garlic shoots

DRESSING

¼ cup (45 g) almond butter

¼ cup (59 ml) fresh lemon juice

¼ cup (59 ml) water

1 tsp ginger powder

1 tsp miso paste

Put the tomatoes in a dehydrator for 1 to 2 hours at 115°F (46°C) until they get
juicy and their skin gets slightly wrinkly. You can also use your oven at its lowest
temperature until the same thing happens, around 30 to 60 minutes.

To make the dressing: blend all the ingredients together until smooth. Toss the
dressing with all the greens and put them in a large bowl.

Now you have some choices to make. You can either leave this dish all raw and it'll
taste pretty good, or you can steam the beets and it'll become an A+. Sooooo: peel
and cut the beets into ¼-inch (6-mm) slices and steam for 10 minutes, or until they
become slightly translucent and have softened a little. Otherwise leave it raw and slice
thinly on a mandolin slicer or by hand.

Throw everything together and eat!

BROCCOLI PESTO

with Swiss Chard, Sliced Asparagus, Radish, Beets + Sunflower Seeds

Asparagus is surprisingly yummy when left raw. The broccoli pesto isn't really pesto, but I didn't know what else to call it. If you want it to be more like pesto, use pine nuts instead of Brazil nuts and add some extra virgin olive oil.

BROCCOLI PESTO

2 cups (459 g) chopped broccoli

¾ cup (114 g) Brazil nuts, soaked for 4 hours

2 tbsp (28 g) miso paste

3 tbsp (44 ml) maple syrup

3 tbsp (44 ml) apple cider vinegar

¼ cup (10 g) packed basil leaves

2 peeled garlic cloves

1 tbsp (14 g) chunk peeled ginger

⅓ cup (79 ml) water, or more as needed

ASPARAGUS

10 asparagus stalks

1 tbsp (15 ml) gluten-free tamari

1 tbsp (15 ml) extra virgin olive oil (optional)

1 tbsp (15 ml) maple syrup

BEET SAUCE (OPTIONAL)

1 small red beet

1 cup (200 g) Broccoli Pesto

¼ cup (59 ml) coconut milk

SALAD

4 small beets

4 small radishes

3 cups (108 g) Swiss chard

3 cups (90 g) spinach

¼ cup (10 g) fresh parsley

¼ cup (20 g) sunflower seeds

To make the pesto: blend everything until smooth, adding water as needed. Adjust according to taste. Set aside.

To prepare the asparagus: slice all the asparagus in half lengthwise on a mandolin or by hand. Toss them with the tamari, olive oil and syrup and leave in the dehydrator at 115°F (46°C) for 30 minutes to soften. Or leave it raw, if you'd like.

If you wanna make the beet sauce: just blend a beet with some of the broccoli pesto and coconut milk. It's fun to have another color in the dish.

To prepare the salad: slice the beets and radishes thinly on mandolin or by hand. Chop the greens into bite size pieces.

Throw the pesto onto the salad ingredients and mix well. Decorate the plates with the beet sauce (if you made it), asparagus and salad.

ONION CORN BREAD SANDWICH

with Avocado + Spinach Filling

I love this bread! It's chewy, soft and flavorful. If you want it to be crispier, toast it for a sec before you make the sandwiches. Technically it won't be raw anymore, but c'mooooon, we're all chill here. The filling is essentially my fave salad (at the moment), but as usual, feel free to add whatever else your (hopefully) optimally functioning heart desires.

BREAD

½ cup (80 g) whole flax seeds

½ cup (64 g) sunflower seeds

1 cup (151 g) chopped onion

1 cup (151 g) sweet corn kernels

2 chopped tomatoes

¾ tsp cumin powder

¾ tsp coriander powder

To make the bread: grind the flax and sunflower seeds into a flour using a high-speed blender (if you don't have a blender, ignore this step and use the seeds whole). Add the seed flour to the veggies and spices in a food processor and process everything together until you get a moist, chunky paste. Spread this evenly onto dehydrator tray(s) about a ⅓-inch (a little less than 1-cm) thick and "bake" for 3 to 4 hours at 115°F (46°C). Cut into squares, gently flip over and finish "baking" for another 3 hours or so, until each square can hold its shape and is totally dry but still pliable. It should be like dense, chewy bread.

FILLING

3 tbsp (45 ml) fresh lemon juice

5 cups (120 g) baby spinach leaves

1 avocado

¼ cup (12 g) green onion

½ cup (170 g) purple cabbage

½ cup (80 g) cherry tomatoes

¼ cup (10 g) basil leaves

½ tsp garlic powder

¼ tsp Himalayan salt

⅛ tsp black pepper

To make the filling: mix the lemon juice with the spinach. Cut up the avocado and then mash it into the spinach leaves, creating a creamy dressing. Chop the green onions, cabbage and tomatoes and add them to the filling mixture. Stir everything with the rest of the filling ingredients until combined.

Scoop the filling onto a piece of bread and then put another piece of bread on top. Eat! Warning: it gets a little messy, but that doesn't stop the deliciousness.

COOKED

Ah, the comfort of a warm plate. Although I always emphasize the importance of eating plenty of raw fruits and veggies, I still love cooking food. It can bring out flavors and textures that otherwise we'd never be able to enjoy. Some fruits and veggies are actually more nutritious when they are lightly cooked. For example: certain nutrients in tomatoes are more easily absorbed by our digestive system when they're cooked. I believe that eating a variety of colorful plant foods allows us to be our very best, and when cooking these foods opens up those possibilities even more. I live for my smoothies and green juices in the daytime, but usually when dinner rolls around my stomach is growling for something more substantial, so I turn to the filling, nourishing meals in this chapter. Let's get cookin'.

> NOTE. For all intents and purposes, every recipe In this chapter serves 2 to 3.

MAC + CHEEZE

The Healthy Way

Need I say more?

MAC

2 cups (232 g) uncooked whole grain, gluten-free pasta

CHEEZE

2 medium yams

2 tsp (10 ml) apple cider vinegar

2 tsp (10 ml) maple syrup

1 tsp sea salt

3 to 4 peeled garlic cloves, as desired

2 tbsp (21 g) nutritional yeast

¼ cup (45 g) cashew butter

1 cup (237 ml) water, as needed

1 tsp tumeric

½ tsp black pepper

Cook the pasta according to the package directions.

Wash and peel the yams, then cut into ½-inch (13-mm) pieces and steam for 10 minutes or until tender. Set aside a handful of pieces. Blend the rest of the yam with the remaining cheeze sauce ingredients until the mixture is smooth and thick enough to hold its shape, adding water as needed.

Mix the cheesy sauce into your pasta along with the few pieces of yam you set aside, sprinkle on some cracked black pepper and indulge happily! It's all good!

THE GREEN BOWL

Steamed Broccoli, Green Lentils, Baked Zucchini + Basil Pesto

All hail chlorophyll! It's what makes leaves and veggies green… and it's really good for you. I adore baking zucchini because it only needs about 20 minutes in the oven before it becomes tender, delicate and juicy. The pesto in this recipe is amazing (in other words: put it on everything).

BAKED ZUCCHINI

1 medium zucchini

1 tsp fresh lemon juice

½ tsp Herbes de Provence

¼ tsp sea salt (optional)

BASIL PESTO

1 cup (125 g) raw pine nuts

3 cups (121 g) fresh basil

¼ cup (37 g) pistachios

¼ tsp Himalayan salt (optional)

2 peeled garlic cloves

1 tbsp (15 ml) apple cider vinegar

¼ cup (59 ml) water

3 cups (689 g) broccoli florets

2 tsp (10 ml) apple cider vinegar

1 ½ cups (302 g) cooked green lentils

To prepare the zucchini: preheat the oven to 350°F (177°C). Slice the zucchini into disks, then lightly coat in the lemon juice, herbs and salt (if using) and bake for 20 to 30 minutes until they are tender and juicy.

To make the pesto: put all the ingredients, except the water, into a food processor and pulse until it's a crumby mixture. You can leave it like this or add water in 1 tablespoon (15 ml) amounts until it becomes creamier.

To prepare the broccoli: steam for 10 minutes or until it becomes a vibrant green color.

Stir the apple cider vinegar into the lentils.

Layer the bottom of a bowl with the lentils and cover with broccoli, zucchini and a scoop of pesto; add extra basil leaves if you want. Enjoy!

I LOVE YU CHOY

Steamed Greens with Brown Rice, Beets, Black Beans + Ginger Almond Sauce

Cannot. Stop. Eating. This.

GINGER ALMOND SAUCE

¼ cup (59 ml) water

¼ cup (45 g) almond butter

1 tsp garlic powder

1 tsp ginger powder

1 tbsp (15 ml) apple cider vinegar

½ tsp maple syrup

¼ tsp sea salt

1 cup (211 g) uncooked brown rice

1 large red beet

1 green onion

4 cups (144 g) yu choy

2 cups (440 g) cooked black beans

To make the ginger almond sauce: blend everything until smooth. Yum.

Cook the rice according to the package directions.

Wash the veggies. Peel and chop the beet into ½-inch (13-mm) pieces and slice the green onion. Steam the yu choy with the beets for 10 minutes, or until they're tender and vibrant green and red.

Fill your serving bowls with the rice and beans, then top off with the steamed veg and some chopped green onion. Drizzle in the almond sauce and nom it up.

SOBA NOODLES

with Avocado, Carrot Ribbons, Shredded Spinach + Maple Miso Glaze

So fresh and simple! I love soba noodles; their texture, flavor and health benefits make me moan, "UGH YES." Soba noodles are made from gluten-free, protein-rich buckwheat. Buckwheat also has a nice amount of B vitamins for brain maintenance. The sauce in this recipe is delicate and light, but adds an undertone of sweet tanginess that pairs perfectly with the savory noodles and crunchy, juicy veggies.

GLAZE

2 tsp (9 g) miso paste

2 tsp (10 ml) maple syrup

1 tbsp (15 ml) fresh lemon juice

3 to 4 tbsp (44 to 59 ml) vegetable broth or water

1 peeled garlic clove

½ tsp chunk peeled ginger

NOODLES

2 cups (180 g) uncooked soba noodles

VEGGIES

1 medium carrot

½ avocado

1 cup (30 g) shredded spinach

1 tbsp (10 g) black sesame seeds (optional)

To make the glaze: blend all the ingredients together until smooth; it should be the consistency of cream. If it's too watery, add 1 tablespoon (9 g) of miso paste. If it's too thick, add 1 tablespoon (15 ml) of water.

To prepare the noodles: cook according to the package directions.

To prepare the veggies: using a mandolin slicer, spiral slicer or simply a cheese grater, shred the carrot into thin slices. Slice the avocado meat thinly lengthwise.

Toss the noodles with the spinach, carrot shreds and the glaze, then garnish with the avocado slices and sesame seeds (if using). Woo!

PUMPKIN SOUP

with Potatoes, Pumpkin Seeds, Leeks + Coconut Milk

Sometimes I host public vegan potlucks with a friend of mine, and all the nearby herbivore-ish peeps come out to enjoy delicious dishes. A few months ago, a lovely Austrian couple came to one and brought with them a delicious, creamy pumpkin soup. It was my favorite item that evening. This is my version.

SOUP

2 cups (360 g) russet potatoes, chopped into ½-inch (13-mm) cubes

3 cups (539 g), pumpkin chopped into ½-inch (13-mm) cubes

14 ½ oz (400 ml) coconut milk (about 1 can)

2 garlic cloves

1 tsp sea salt

¼ tsp black pepper

TOPPINGS

2 tbsp (10 g) pumpkin seeds

¼ cup (12 g) leeks, thinly sliced

Preheat the oven to 350°F (177°C). Bake the potatoes and pumpkin for 30 minutes or until tender all the way through. Throw it in a blender with the coconut milk, garlic, salt and pepper. Blend until smooth. You can add more coconut milk or water if it's too thick, and add more salt if you want to.

Top with the pumpkin seeds and thinly sliced leeks.

JASMINE RICE
with Edamame, Black Beans + Salsa

Sometimes I get too caught up in what I think my recipes should be and forget that my everyday eats are not only the easiest to make, but also da best. That's why I eat 'em everyday. Duh. So then I remind myself that I don't need to come up with complicated, impressive-sounding food for my blog or this cookbook; it's more natural and honest to simply photograph and share the recipes for what I eat on the reg. This is an example, and it's sooo gooooood. *Crying with joy.* It's fun to add steamed beets to this because the rice turns pink.

SALSA

2 cups (322 g) roughly chopped tomatoes

¼ cup (50 g) finely chopped onion

3 peeled, minced garlic cloves

2 tbsp (30 ml) fresh lemon juice

¼ cup (10 g) basil leaves

Salt and pepper, to taste

2 cups (303 g) uncooked edamame

4 cups (644 g) cooked jasmine rice

2 cups (440 g) cooked black beans

To make the salsa: throw all ingredients together, adding salt and pepper as you desire. You could use cilantro instead of basil if you like. Your salsa should be pretty juicy thanks to the tomato and lemon juices, but this is a good thing—it'll soak into the rice. Mmm.

Steam the edamame for 8 minutes and then shell all the soybeans out.

Layer the rice in bowls and top off with salsa, black beans, soybeans and a little more black pepper if you like.

SWEET POTATO SLICES

with Lime-Spritzed Baby Greens + Corn

I love meals like this. They come together in no time, they are very filling and nourishing, and they're pretty low in fat as well (in case you care about that kinda thing). One of my favorite foods is the glorious sweet potato, so this recipe is a real treat.

1 large sweet potato

2 tbsp (30 ml) fresh lemon juice

1 tsp coconut oil

SALAD

1 cup (151 g) sweet corn kernels

3 cups (60 g) baby greens

1 tbsp (15 ml) fresh lime juice

¼ tsp sea salt

¼ tsp black pepper

1 tsp dulse flakes (optional)

To prepare the sweet potato: preheat the oven to 350°F (177°C). Wash and scrub the sweet potato gently. Slice it in half lengthwise, then slice each half into ½-inch (13-mm)-thick slices widthwise (so you end up with a bunch of half-moon shaped slices). Put the slices in a large bowl and toss with the lemon juice and coconut oil until evenly coated. Bake for 20 minutes, flip all the slices over then bake for another 20 minutes, or until tender all the way through (check with a fork).

To make the salad: steam the corn kernels until soft, about 5 minutes. Toss all the ingredients together, including the steamed corn. Serve with your baked sweet potato slices and enjoy!

CREAMY CAULIFLOWER SAUCE

with Rice Noodles

Think of this as healthy and low-fat fettuccine alfredo. I love serving it with basil and chili flakes, and whatever other fresh veg I have in the kitchen at the time.

2 cups (180 g) uncooked rice noodles

SAUCE

1 small cauliflower head

2 tbsp (28 g) miso paste

2 tbsp (15 g) nutritional yeast

2 tbsp (22 g) cashew butter

1 tbsp (15 ml) fresh lemon juice

½ cup (118 ml) water

Cook the noodles according to the package directions. Rinse with cold water and set aside.

Roughly chop the cauliflower and steam for 10 minutes or until tender. In a blender, blend the cauliflower with the rest of the ingredients until smooth. Taste and adjust accordingly, add a little salt and/or pepper if you like.

Toss the noodles with the sauce until evenly coated then enjoy!

SAUTÉED ASPARAGUS

with Marinated Mushrooms + Almonds

I didn't think I even liked asparagus that much until I tasted this. If you like vinegary flavors, then you will love this recipe. The asparagus is sautéed in apple cider vinegar, and the result is tangy and delicious. The three different textures (meaty, tender, crunchy) combined together are on point as well.

MARINATED MUSHROOMS

2 cups (118 g) baby shiitake mushrooms

1 tsp gluten-free tamari

1 tsp fresh lemon juice

1 tsp extra virgin olive oil

SAUTÉED ASPARAGUS

1 bunch asparagus

1 tbsp (15 ml) extra virgin olive oil

1 tbsp (15 ml) apple cider vinegar

1 tsp maple syrup

1 to 2 tsp (5 to 10 ml) gluten-free tamari, as desired

¼ tsp black pepper

½ tsp dried savory

ALMONDS

3 tbsp (11 g) almonds

1 tsp black sesame seeds

To marinate the mushrooms: toss them with the tamari, lemon juice and olive oil and let them sit in a bowl in a warm spot for 30 minutes, or bake them gently at 200°F (93°C) for 20 minutes. If your oven doesn't go that low, just use the lowest temperature and keep an eye on the food since you may need to take it out a few minutes early.

To sauté the asparagus: cut off the tips of the ends and wash the stalks. Toss the stalks with the rest of the ingredients, then on medium-low heat in a pan, sauté for 10 minutes until the asparagus becomes darker green and tender. Bite one to see if you like them. If they're still too crunchy for you, sauté for another 5 minutes or so.

To prepare the almonds: you should have leftover juices in the pan that you sautéed the asparagus in. Mix the almonds with the pan juices, along with the sesame seeds. If all the juices cooked away, simply mix the almonds in a little lemon juice and salt, along with the sesame seeds.

Serve the asparagus, mushrooms and almonds beside each other on a plate. Suh-weet.

BAKED EGGPLANT

with Rosemary Salt, Savory + Cilantro Sauce

So tender and juicy! This recipe is very easy and pretty quick too. A great choice when you want something comforting, nourishing and filling. Tip: this would be amazing with the falafel recipe on page 166.

BAKED EGGPLANT

1 globe eggplant

2 tsp (10 ml) coconut oil

1 tsp dried savory

½ tsp rosemary-infused sea salt or plain sea salt

1 tbsp (15 ml) fresh lemon juice

CILANTRO SAUCE

½ cup (237 ml) water

1 tbsp (14 g) tahini

½ cup (20 g) fresh cilantro

¼ cup (10 g) fresh parsley

½ tsp sea salt

1 peeled garlic clove

1 tsp chunk peeled ginger

To bake the eggplant: preheat the oven to 350°F (177°C). Wash the eggplant, then cut off the top and slice it in half lengthwise. Mix the coconut oil with the rest of the ingredients and rub this mixture onto the two eggplant halves. Bake, with their dark sides facing up, for 30 minutes or until tender all the way through.

To make the cilantro sauce: blend all the ingredients until smooth. If you want it less watery, add 1 tablespoon (14 g) more of tahini, and a ½ cup (20 g) of cilantro. Serve each eggplant slice drizzled with the sauce.

WARMING MISO SOUP

with Leeks + Ginger

I had never tried leeks until I made this recipe, and I now realize the error of my ways: I should have been eating them from day one. They are like onions, but better. All you have to do to coax out their amazing flavor is sauté them for a few minutes until they get tender. I added finely chopped ginger for some natural warmth. This is a great recipe for winter, and if you want to make it more filling, serve with some brown rice or quinoa.

LEEKS + GINGER

1 tbsp (15 ml) coconut oil

1 tsp gluten-free tamari

3 tbsp (44 ml) water, as needed

1 tbsp (14 g) chunk peeled ginger, finely chopped

2 cups (260 g) leeks, chopped into 1" (13 mm) pieces

SOUP

1 tbsp (14 g) miso paste

2 cups (473 ml) hot water

To prepare the leeks and ginger: heat the oil in a pan on medium-low heat. Add the tamari and 1 tablespoon (15 ml) of water. Add the ginger and leeks to the pan and sauté for 10 minutes, adding 1 to 3 tablespoons (15 to 44 ml) of water if the pan gets dry, until the leeks are tender. Taste to see if you like them, and if they are still too hard, cook for another 5 minutes or so.

To make the soup: blend the miso with the water until smooth. Pour into bowls then add the sautéed leeks and ginger. Perfection.

BAKED YAMS

with Quinoa, Sprouts, Spicy Tofu + Chili Almond Sauce

I don't eat tofu that often (in fact, I think this is the only tofu recipe in here), but I like it a lot. I just get distracted by all the pretty colors at the farmer's market and usually forget about the poor lil guy. But when I am running low on fresh produce, tofu comes to the rescue and fills my tummy. It soaks up the flavors of whatever you cook it with, so it's great sautéed with yummy sauces like we're gonna do in this recipe.

2 medium yams

SPICY TOFU

¾ cup (170 g) firm tofu

1 tsp chili powder

½ tsp ground coffee beans

1 tsp gluten-free tamari

½ tsp ginger powder

1 tsp coconut oil

1 cup (211 g) uncooked quinoa

CHILI ALMOND SAUCE

3 tbsp (34 g) almond butter

3 tbsp (45 ml) water

½ tsp sea salt

½ tsp chili powder

¼ cup (10 g) sunflower sprouts

To bake the yams: preheat the oven to 350°F (177°C). Wash and scrub the yams, then slice each one in half lengthwise. Bake for 30 to 40 minutes, or until they are tender all the way through and bubbling around the edges. So sexy.

To prepare the tofu: slice into 2-inch (5-cm)-wide pieces then rub with the rest of the ingredients. Sauté in a pan on medium-low heat for 5 minutes on each side. If you have extra oil in the pan when they're done, you can rub it on your yams before eating.

To prepare the quinoa: cook according to the package directions.

To make the almond sauce: stir the ingredients together, but add just 1 or 2 tablespoons (15 to 30 ml) of water to start. If it's still too thick, add 1 tablespoon (15 ml) of water at a time until it's smooth and saucy.

Serve everything in a bowl with the quinoa on the bottom, followed by the yams and tofu, then garnish with the sprouts and a drizzle of the almond sauce.

CREAM OF CARROT SOUP

with Fennel Seed, Paprika + Thyme

I always forget how much I love soup—until I make a bowl of soup. This is perfect for a cold, rainy day, made with fresh carrots from the farmer's market or your own garden. Option: switch out the potato for yam.

2 ½ cups (592 ml) water

2 cups (303 g) chopped carrots

⅓ cup (51 g) chopped potatoes

3 peeled garlic cloves

1 small onion

1 tbsp (14 g) chunk peeled ginger

1 tsp dried thyme, plus more for garnish

1 tsp paprika powder, plus more for garnish

½ tsp fennel seeds, plus more for garnish

¼ tsp black pepper, plus more for garnish

2 tbsp (30 ml) extra virgin olive oil (optional)

1 tsp sea salt

Throw everything into a pot, except the olive oil and salt, and bring to a boil. Reduce to a simmer and let everything cook in the water for 10 to 15 minutes, or until the onion is falling apart and tender and the potatoes are at least soft enough to poke through with a fork.

Transfer everything into a blender, adding the olive oil and salt now, and blend until smooth. Adjust according to taste, adding more salt or other spices if desired.

Pour into bowls and garnish with cracked black pepper, more olive oil, fennel, paprika and thyme, and perhaps a sprig of basil or other fresh greens. Curl up with a blanket and enjoy!

CREAMY BUTTERNUT SQUASH

with Sage, Cranberry Jam + Micro Greens

Ah, the fall harvest. Here in British Columbia, we get squash all autumn and winter, so it symbolizes the season for me. I am keeping it simple in this recipe by just baking the squash in the oven with some herbs and lemon juice. It pairs perfectly with the sweetly tart cranberry jam, and you get some fresh, crisp flavor from the radish sprouts (which you can grow yourself by a window any time of year or pick up in the grocery store).

BUTTERNUT SQUASH

1 medium butternut squash

2 tbsp (30 ml) fresh lemon juice

1 tbsp (15 ml) coconut oil

1 tbsp (3 g) finely chopped sage leaves

1 tsp dried thyme

¼ tsp black pepper

½ tsp Himalayan salt

CRANBERRY JAM

1 cup (99 g) cranberries

⅓ cup (79 ml) orange juice

½ tsp orange zest

1 tbsp (12 g) coconut sugar (optional)

½ cup (20 g) radish sprouts

To prepare the butternut squash: preheat the oven to 350°F (177°C) then cut the squash into 1-inch (2.5-cm) cubes (removing the seeds as needed) and mix with the lemon juice, coconut oil, herbs, pepper and salt until evenly coated. Bake for 30 minutes, then flip all the cubes over and bake for another 30 minutes, or until they are tender and a fork can easily go all the way through when you poke them.

To make the cranberry jam: put the cranberries, orange juice and orange zest into a sauce pan on medium heat and bring the juice to a simmer. Reduce to low heat and continue stirring occasionally for 10 to 15 minutes until the cranberries have burst and softened and the mixture is thick and pinkish red. Take off the heat and let the jam cool for 20 minutes. If you'd like it sweeter, stir in some coconut sugar.

Serve the butternut squash on a plate with cranberry jam, topped off with radish sprouts.

MY FAVE DINNER

Sweet Potato with Tahini, Lemon + Black Pepper

I eat this nearly every night, and it never gets old. As I continue exploring the beautiful, colorful world of wholesome eating and living, I find my palate evolving constantly. These days, I often don't need or want salt or oil on my meals. My tastebuds have learned to appreciate the simple flavors of the actual plants, and it's a very pleasing experience. If you want to add salt, go ahead, but consider using less than normal, and in time you'll become more sensitive (in a good way) to the food you're eating. When you use high-quality ingredients, you don't have to do much to 'em. This is why I advocate buying organic and locally grown produce; it tastes better!

4 large sweet potatoes

4 tbsp (56 g) tahini

3 tbsp (44 ml) fresh lemon juice

¾ tsp black pepper

Preheat the oven to 350°F (177°C). Wash and scrub the sweet potatoes, then poke holes in them with a fork to help them ventilate while they cook. Bake for 40 minutes, then check with a fork to see if they are tender all the way through. If not, flip them over and bake for another 10 or 15 minutes.

Serve on plates: slice them open in the middle, mash them a little with a fork, then drizzle on the tahini, spritz on the lemon juice and sprinkle the black pepper. Perfection.

WINTER MELON SOUP

with Ginger, Cilantro + Shimeji Mushrooms

I picked up some winter melon without knowing what it was because I like making up recipes with new ingredients, and after some internet searching I discovered that it is the star of a traditional Chinese soup. This is my version. Winter melon reminds me of daikon, but with a milder flavor. I love how tender the melon becomes when cooked long enough; it practically melts in your mouth.

2 tbsp (29 g) chunk peeled ginger

1 tbsp (15 ml) coconut oil (optional)

3 cups (710 ml) vegetable broth

2 cups (199 g) peeled winter melon, cut into 1-inch (2.5-cm) cubes

1 cup (59 g) brown shimeji mushrooms

½ cup (20 g) cilantro

¼ tsp chili flakes (optional)

Slice the ginger thinly, then warm it up with the coconut oil in a pot over medium heat for 1 minute (if you're not using coconut oil, just add the ginger along with the broth).

Add the broth and melon and simmer for 20 minutes. Add the mushrooms and keep simmering for another 10 minutes or until the melon is translucent and tender enough to easily stick a fork through.

Garnish with cilantro and if you like it spicy, add some chili flakes.

RICE NOODLES

with Peas, Mint, Basil + Peanut Lime Sauce

This recipe is refreshing and comforting all at once. After I photographed it, I was planning on leaving it for Jack to eat later, but once I had a bite I couldn't stop (sorry, lover). Feel free to use more lime juice in the peanut sauce if you like.

PEANUT LIME SAUCE

2 tbsp (22 g) peanut butter

2 tbsp (22 g) almond butter

2 peeled garlic cloves

2 tsp (10 ml) fresh lime juice

1 tbsp (15 ml) gluten-free tamari

3 tbsp (44 ml) water

4 fresh mint leaves

4 fresh basil leaves

1 cup (151 g) peas

2 cups (180 g) uncooked rice noodles

1 tbsp (3 g) chopped fresh mint leaves

2 tbsp (5 g) chopped fresh basil leaves

To make the sauce: blend all the ingredients together until smooth, adding more water if you need to.

To prepare the peas: steam for 10 minutes or until they are a vibrant green color.

To prepare the noodles: cook the noodles according to the directions on the package, then rinse in cold water and toss in the sauce. Add the peas to the noodles and garnish with the mint and basil. Enjoy!

RAMEN NOODLES

with Baby Bok Choy, Fresh Turmeric + Ginger Broth

This recipe is great for keeping away colds and making you feel happy in general. There's just something special about a bowl of ramen noodles served up with vibrant veg in a steamy broth, am I right? My dad loves this with peanuts and mushrooms on top (he's got good taste). Add tofu or beans for extra umph.

1 tbsp (15 ml) coconut oil

2 peeled garlic cloves

1 tbsp (14 g) chunk peeled ginger

1 tbsp (14 g) chunk peeled turmeric

2 tbsp (28 g) miso paste

5 cups (1.2 l) water

2 cups (180 g) uncooked whole grain, gluten-free ramen noodles

2 heads baby bok choy

2 nori sheets, cut into thin strips

½ cup (20 g) fresh cilantro

Sea salt, as desired

Melt the coconut oil in a pot over medium-low heat. Slice the garlic, ginger and turmeric thinly and add them to the pot, sautéing for 3 minutes, then add the miso and stir it into the oil as best you can. Add the water and bring to boil. Add the noodles and bok choy, lower the heat and cook everything for 5 to 8 minutes or until the noodles are done and the bok choy is vibrantly green and tender.

Serve in bowls, garnished with the nori and cilantro, adding salt to taste. Mmm.

TRICOLOR QUINOA

with Tahini, Steamed Beets, Carrots + Peas

This is a recipe that comes together quickly. It's very simple and also quite low in fat, since no oil is required to cook the veggies or quinoa. I love meals like this when I want something lighter for dinner or lunch that will still give my body all it needs to thrive.

1 cup (211 g) uncooked tricolor quinoa

2 golden beets

4 large carrots

1 cup (151 g) peas

3 tbsp (42 g) tahini

¼ tsp sea salt

¼ tsp black pepper

½ tsp white sesame seeds

½ tsp black sesame seeds

Cook the quinoa according to the package directions.

Peel the beets and carrots then steam them for 10 minutes along with the peas, or until everything is vibrantly colored and tender.

Serve the vegetables on a bed of quinoa, drizzle with tahini then sprinkle with salt, pepper and the sesame seeds.

SWEET + SOUR BOK CHOY

with Whole-Grain Miso Noodles

Bok choy looks sexy when you sauté it. You can sub in any other leafy green veggie if you want, and try this with rice!

2 cups (180 g) uncooked whole grain, gluten-free noodles

MISO SAUCE

1 tbsp (14 g) miso paste

1 tbsp (15 ml) water

1 tsp fresh lemon juice

1 tsp coconut sugar

2 peeled garlic cloves

5 to 6 sun-dried tomato slices

SWEET + SOUR BOK CHOY

6 heads bok choy

1 tbsp (15 ml) extra virgin olive oil

1 tbsp (15 ml) maple syrup

1 tbsp (15 ml) rice vinegar

1 tbsp (15 ml) gluten-free tamari

Black basil leaves (optional)

To prepare the miso noodles: cook the noodles according to the package directions.

Blend the miso sauce ingredients, except for the tomatoes, until smooth. Mix the sauce into the noodles along with the tomato slices and set aside.

To prepare the sweet + sour bok choy: wash the bok choy heads then slice each in half, lengthwise. Heat the oil in a pan over medium-low heat. Add the rest of the ingredients to the pan and sauté the bok choy for 8 to 10 minutes, with the cut-side down. After 8 minutes, check to see if the cut-side is brown. If not, continue cooking until they are.

Serve beside the noodles and enjoy! I garnished mine with black basil leaves.

RED KURI SQUASH

with Basmati Rice + Baby Spinach Tossed in Ginger Lemon Dressing

Lemony greens + baked squash = heaven in my mouth.

SQUASH

6 cups (750 g) red kuri squash, chopped into 1-inch (2.5-cm) cubes

2 tbsp (30 ml) fresh lemon juice

1 tbsp (15 ml) coconut oil (optional)

¼ tsp Himalayan salt

¼ tsp black pepper

2 tsp (1 g) dried basil

GINGER LEMON DRESSING

1 tbsp (14 g) chunk peeled ginger

2 tbsp (30 ml) fresh lemon juice

1 tsp maple syrup

2 tbsp (30 ml) water

1 tsp almond butter

1 cup (211 g) uncooked basmati rice

3 cups (90 g) baby spinach leaves, washed

To prepare the squash: preheat the oven to 400°F (205°C). Toss the squash with the other ingredients and bake for 25 minutes or until tender and browning on the edges.

To make the dressing: blend everything together until smooth. If you'd like it to be sweeter, add 1 teaspoon of maple syrup. If it's too watery, add 1 teaspoon of almond butter.

To prepare the rice: cook according to the package directions.

Toss the baby spinach leaves in the dressing, and serve alongside the rice and squash. Oh, baby!

PEAS + GREENS

Paprika-Baked Yams with Spinach + Peas

Another ridiculously simple yet delicious recipe. Plants are #winning.

BAKED YAMS

2 yams

1 tsp paprika powder

1 tsp fresh lime juice

SALAD

4 cups (120 g) baby spinach leaves

2 tbsp (30 ml) fresh lime juice

1 tsp maple syrup

1 tsp sea salt

2 cups (303 g) peas

1 avocado

½ tsp black sesame seeds

To bake the yams: preheat the oven to 350°F (177°C). Wash and scrub the yams. Cut into ½-inch (13-mm) cubes and toss with the paprika and lime juice. Bake for 25 to 30 minutes or until tender.

To make the salad: toss the spinach with lime juice, maple syrup, salt and peas. Serve with the yam, avocado and sprinkle on some sesame seeds.

WHOLE FOOD PROTEINS

Baked Potatoes with Golden Beets, Tahini Greens + White Navy Beans

I suggest getting your taters from the farmer's market. Potatoes are one of the most contaminated commercially grown foods, so it's a smart move for the planet and your own health to get them local and organic. They taste way better that way too. This recipe is full of healthy proteins for your body since there's protein in all plant foods (which is why getting enough protein on a plant-based diet is a non-issue).

6 red Viking potatoes

1 golden beet

3 cups (108 g) collard greens

GREEN TAHINI SAUCE

2 tbsp (28 g) tahini

½ tsp sea salt

1 tsp apple cider vinegar

¼ cup (10 g) cilantro or basil leaves

¼ cup (59 ml) water

2 cups (512 g) cooked white navy beans

To prepare the potatoes: preheat the oven to 350°F (177°C). Wrap the potatoes tightly in tin foil and bake for 40 to 60 minutes, or until a fork easily goes all the way through them. Cut into wedges.

Peel the beet and slice thinly on a mandolin slicer. Cut the spine out of the collard greens (it sounds so gruesome, but I don't know how else to say it), and then slice the leaves into short strips.

To make the green tahini sauce: blend all the ingredients until smooth.

Toss some of the sauce with the collard greens. Put the greens, potatoes, beet slices and beans into a bowl and drizzle on the rest of the sauce.

ONE-POT VEGGIE NOODLE SOUP

with Miso Broth

Perfect for a rainy day… that's what I think, anyway. Honestly, I wasn't trying to make that rhyme.

4 large carrots

3 cups (201 g) kale leaves

MISO BROTH

6 cups (1.4 l) water

5 tbsp (70 g) miso paste

1 cup (116 g) uncooked whole grain, gluten-free pasta

3 peeled garlic cloves

Slice the carrots into ¼-inch (6-mm) pieces, and if you have big kale leaves, tear them up into pieces that are no larger than your hand.

To make the miso broth: blend 1 cup (237 ml) of the water with the miso, then mix it with the rest of the water.

Bring the miso broth to a boil then add the pasta, cooking for 2 minutes before adding the carrots and garlic. After 5 minutes, add the kale. As soon as you add the kale, turn off the heat and take the pot off the stove. Enjoy!

STEAMED ASPARAGUS

with Red Rice, Mushrooms, Nori + Thick Tomato Sauce

Colorful and good for ya.

TOMATO SAUCE

2 small yams

5 to 6 slices sun-dried tomatoes, soaked in 2 tbsp (30 ml) water

½ cup (118 ml) water

1 tbsp (14 g) tahini

1 tsp sea salt

½ cup (105 g) uncooked red rice

1 bunch asparagus

1 cup (59 g) brown shimeji mushrooms

1 nori sheet

To make the sauce: peel the yams and cut into ½-inch (13-mm) slices, then steam them until soft, about 8 minutes. Blend the steamed yams together with the rest of the sauce ingredients. It will be pretty thick. Adjust according to preference, adding more salt or anything else you like (garlic, miso paste, ginger, etc.)

Cook the rice according to the package directions

Steam the asparagus with the mushrooms for 10 minutes, or until the asparagus is tender and vibrantly green. Shred the nori sheet. Mix the steamed mushrooms and the nori shreds into the rice. Plate with a spoonful of the sauce alongside the rice and asparagus.

ACORN SQUASH

with Romanesco Broccoli + Creamy Ginger Almond Gravy

Fun facts about the ingredients in this recipe: romanesco broccoli looks like it was designed by an artist who likes LSD (I mean that in a good way); squash is delicious and really healthy; and the gravy would make a dirty shoe taste pretty decent (maybe).

BAKED ACORN SQUASH

1 acorn squash

1 tbsp (15 ml) extra virgin olive oil

1 tbsp (15 ml) fresh lemon juice

¼ tsp black pepper

½ tsp Himalayan salt

ROASTED SQUASH SEEDS

Seeds from the squash

½ tsp garam masala powder

1 head romanesco broccoli

CREAMY GINGER ALMOND GRAVY

¼ cup (45 g) almond butter

1 tbsp (14 g) chunk peeled ginger

3 tbsp (44 ml) fresh lemon juice

¼ cup (59 ml) water

½ tsp chili powder

To prepare the squash: preheat the oven to 350°F (177°C), then cut the squash into 1-inch (2.5-cm) thick slices (removing the seeds as you go). Toss the slices in a bowl with the rest of the ingredients until they are evenly coated. Bake for 30 minutes, then flip over and bake for another 20 minutes or until they are fork-tender.

To roast the seeds: coat them in the garam masala powder and bake for 15 minutes at 350°F (177°C).

To prepare the romanesco broccoli: cut the florets into bite size pieces then steam for 8 to 10 minutes or until slightly tender.

To make the gravy: blend everything until smooth. If it is still too thick, add more water or lemon juice in 1 tablespoon (15 ml) amounts.

Serve the broccoli and squash beside each other, with the gravy drizzled on the broccoli and the squash seeds sprinkled on the squash.

YAM FRIES FOREVER

Unless I am having naked-baked yams for dinner, you can bet this is gonna be on my plate. Sometimes I have both. Always with tahini.

2 large yams

2 large sweet potatoes

1 tsp garlic powder

2 tbsp (30 ml) apple cider vinegar

1 tbsp (2 g) dried basil

½ cup (20 g) fresh basil

¼ cup (56 g) tahini

Preheat your oven to 375°F (191°C). Wash, scrub and then slice the yams and sweet potatoes into fries. Coat with the garlic powder, apple cider vinegar and dried basil then bake for 30 minutes or until they are tender all the way through (try one to find out).

Serve with fresh basil and drizzle in tahini. Nirvana.

RAINBOW PLATE

with Tahini

I would say I'm sorry for covering everything in this cookbook in tahini, but I'm not.

2 large yams

2 tsp (1 g) dried basil

2 tsp (10 ml) apple cider vinegar

2 large heads broccoli

2 cups (303 g) sweet corn

1 large golden beet

2 large carrots

1 small head purple cabbage

3 tbsp (42 g) tahini

Salt and pepper (optional)

Preheat the oven to 350°F (177°C). Wash and scrub the yams, then cut into ½-inch (13-mm) slices. Toss with the basil and apple cider vinegar and bake for 30 to 40 minutes, or until they are tender all the way through. Bake a bit longer if you want them to brown.

Cut the broccoli into florets and steam for 10 minutes, or until tender and vibrantly green. Steam the corn as well, for 10 minutes, or until tender and vibrantly yellow. Shred the beet, carrots and cabbage.

Serve all the veggies on plates, drizzled in tahini. Add salt and pepper if desired.

PENNE PESTO

with Basil + Roasted Grape Tomatoes

Pesto forever. And ever.

1 dry pint (275 g) grape tomatoes

2 cups (232 g) uncooked whole grain, gluten-free penne

PESTO

2 cups (48 g) lightly packed basil leaves

¼ cup (59 ml) water, as needed

½ cup (15 g) pine nuts

¼ tsp Himalayan salt

1 garlic clove

1 cup (24 g) lightly packed basil leaves

Preheat the oven to 350°F (177°C). Cut all the tomatoes in half and bake for 15 to 20 minutes or until they are bubbling and slightly wrinkled.

Cook the pasta according to the package directions.

To make the pesto: blend all the ingredients, except the water, until you reach the desired consistency. Add water as needed (some people like really smooth pesto, I like it kinda chunky). Add more salt if you want.

Toss the pesto with the penne and the remaining cup of basil and serve with the roasted tomatoes.

JAPANESE SWEET POTATOES

with Broccoli, Carrot-Turmeric Sauce + Pumpkin Seeds

This variety of sweet potato is such a treat; they remind me of chestnuts (which I love). And lately I have been craving broccoli hard, so this combo is currently unbeatable.

2 large Japanese sweet potatoes

2 large heads broccoli

CARROT-TURMERIC SAUCE

2 medium carrots

2 tsp (5 g) turmeric powder

¼ tsp Himalayan salt

3 tbsp (34 g) cashew butter

¼ cup (59 ml) water

2 tbsp (10 g) pumpkin seeds

Preheat the oven to 350°F (177°C). Wash and scrub the sweet potatoes, then slice into ½-inch (13-mm)-thick slices and bake for 30 to 40 minutes, or until they are tender all the way through and lightly browning on the bottoms.

Break the broccoli into smaller florets and steam for 10 minutes or until vibrantly green and slightly tender.

To make the carrot-turmeric sauce: blend everything together until smooth, adding more salt or turmeric if you like. If it's too thick, add more cashew butter and water. If it's too thin, add more cashew butter and carrot.

Serve the cooked veggies with the sauce and sprinkle on some pumpkin seeds. Yum.

SPICY BROWN RICE

with Red Kidney Beans + Mashed Avocado

Rice and beans, baby. They go so well together that when I make this recipe I almost feel like the third wheel.

1 tsp turmeric powder

1 tsp paprika powder

1 tsp cumin powder

1 tsp garlic powder

1 tsp sea salt

1 tsp apple cider vinegar

2 cups (322 g) cooked brown rice

1 avocado

1 tsp fresh lime juice

2 cups (512 g) cooked red kidney beans

Black pepper, to taste

Fresh cilantro (optional)

Chili flakes (optional)

Toss the spices, salt and apple cider vinegar with the rice. Mash the avocado with a fork and mix in the lime juice.

Serve the beans, rice and mashed avocado together on plates and sprinkle with a little black pepper if you want. This is really good with fresh cilantro and chili flakes.

COUSCOUS

with Roasted Tomatoes, Yam + Gai Choy

I will never get over roasted tomatoes. They are the life-essence of pizza.

2 large yams

10 small tomatoes

Black pepper, to taste

1 cup (211 g) uncooked gluten-free couscous (or another gluten-free grain)

4 cups (268 g) gai choy

3 tbsp (42 g) tahini

3 tbsp (44 ml) fresh lemon juice

½ tsp sea salt

Preheat the oven to 350°F (177°C). Peel the yams and cut into ½-inch (13-mm) cubes. Bake for 30 minutes (flipping them halfway), or until they are tender all the way through.

Slice all the tomatoes in half, sprinkle with some pepper and bake for 30 minutes, or until they are juicy and bubbling a little.

Cook the couscous according to the package directions. Steam the gai choy for 10 minutes or until vibrantly green and tender (I like to leave some of it raw).

Mix together the yams and the couscous.

Lay out a bed of gai choy, then pile on some couscous and yam mixture, and finally decorate with tomatoes. Drizzle with tahini and lemon juice and sprinkle on some salt.

BLACK BEAN NOODLES

with Yams, Asparagus, Sautéed Mushrooms + Peanut Sauce

This my kind of comfort food. Black bean noodles might be tricky to find in your area, so if you have no luck, just use your fave whole grain pasta, soba noodles or rice.

2 medium yams

3 cups (402 g) asparagus

2 cups (180 g) uncooked black bean noodles

SAUTÉED MUSHROOMS

3 ½ oz (100 g) bunapi mushrooms

2 tsp (10 ml) gluten-free tamari

2 tsp (10 ml) coconut oil

1 tbsp (15 ml) water

2 tsp (10 ml) apple cider vinegar

½ tsp paprika powder

½ tsp turmeric powder

PEANUT SAUCE

¼ cup (45 g) peanut butter

1 tbsp (14 g) miso

1 tbsp (15 ml) fresh lime juice

1 peeled garlic clove

1 tsp chunk peeled ginger

2 tsp (9 ml) water

¼ tsp chili flakes (optional)

Cilantro sprigs (optional)

Wash the veggies. Peel the yams and then chop into ½-inch (13-mm) cubes. Steam for 8 to 10 minutes or until tender and vibrantly orange. Steam the asparagus for 5 to 7 minutes or until tender and vibrantly green. Cook the noodles according to package instructions.

To sauté the 'shrooms: in a pan over medium-low heat, add all the ingredients for the sautéed mushrooms and sauté until the mushrooms are tender, about 10 minutes. If the pan becomes too dry, add more water in 1 teaspoon amounts as needed.

Toss the noodles, yam, asparagus and mushrooms together.

To make the peanut sauce: blend everything, except the chili and cilantro, until smooth. Garnish with chili and cilantro if you want.

Drizzle the sauce over your noodles and veg. Eat it.

BUTTERNUT SQUASH SOUP

with Cinnamon, Coriander + Caraway Seeds

Ridiculously good. You might think cinnamon in soup sounds weird, but try it yourself. You'll see… you'll all see.

SOUP

3 cups (615 g) butternut squash, cut into ½-inch (13-mm) cubes

3 cups (710 ml) coconut milk

1 tsp sea salt

½ tsp caraway seeds

¼ tsp cinnamon powder

½ tsp coriander seeds

GARNISH

4 basil sprigs

⅛ tsp chili flakes

Steam the butternut squash until tender, about 15 minutes. Blend it up with the rest of the soup ingredients until smooth. If you want more salt, add some. If the soup is too thick, add more coconut milk.

Serve with basil leaves and chili flakes.

OIL-FREE BAKED POTATO FRIES

with Thyme + Garlic

Eat as many as you want: potatoes are a super food. Try to get organic taters; otherwise, they are one of the most pesticide-contaminated foods.

6 large russet potatoes

1 tsp sea salt

1 tsp black pepper

3 tbsp (9 g) fresh thyme leaves

2 tsp (5 g) garlic powder

Preheat the oven to 375°F (191°C). Wash and scrub the potatoes (peel them if they're not organic). Slice 'em into fries and arrange on a parchment paper-lined baking pan (you might need more than one pan). Sprinkle on the salt, pepper, thyme and garlic. Bake for 30 minutes or until they start getting brown and crispy. Check one by tasting it, and bake 10 minutes longer if you want.

FREEDOM FALAFEL

with Lemon Pepper Spinach Salad

Hearty, filling, flavorful and so good for you! These are packed with protein and FREE—*Oh, I get the recipe's name now*—from all the stuff your body doesn't want or need so you can enjoy them, get healthy and keep living well.

FALAFEL

1 cup (126 g) uncooked white fava beans, soaked 24 hours in water then rinsed

1 cup (151 g) chopped onion

3 peeled garlic cloves

½ tsp coriander powder

½ tsp cumin powder

¼ tsp sea salt

¼ tsp black pepper

1 cup (40 g) fresh cilantro

1 cup (40 g) fresh parsley

2 tbsp (30 ml) extra virgin olive oil

2 tbsp (28 g) tahini

1 tbsp (10 g) white sesame seeds

SALAD

3 cups (90 g) baby spinach

1 cup (40 g) fresh parsley

1 cup (40 g) fresh cilantro

2 tbsp (30 ml) fresh lemon juice

¼ tsp black pepper

To make the falafel: preheat the oven to 350°F (177°C). Throw all the falafel ingredients, except for the sesame seeds, in your food processor and process until it is evenly combined and like a thick, grainy paste. Form into balls, roll in the sesame seeds and bake for 30 minutes or until they are brown and slightly crispy on the outside.

To make the salad: toss the spinach, parsley and cilantro with the lemon juice and black pepper. Make a bed of this in a bowl, then add on your falafel and enjoy!

PEARL COUSCOUS

with Steamed Asparagus, Sun-Dried Tomato Sauce, Basil + Mint Leaves

This kind of couscous is my all time fave. It's like little balls of pasta… and when is pasta ever a bad thing?

1 cup (116 g) uncooked gluten-free pearl couscous (or another gluten-free grain)

2 cups (269 g) asparagus

1 yellow beet

SUN-DRIED TOMATO SAUCE

½ cup (83 g) sun-dried tomatoes

1 ½ cups (355 ml) water

2 tbsp (28 g) tahini

½ tsp salt

¼ tsp black pepper

½ tsp cinnamon powder

½ tsp paprika powder

½ tsp dried oregano

2 tbsp (5 g) fresh mint leaves

2 tbsp (5 g) fresh basil leaves

Cook the couscous according to the package directions. Steam the asparagus for 10 minutes or until its tender and vibrantly green. Peel the beet, slice into ½-inch (13-mm) pieces and steam for 10 to 12 minutes or until tender.

To make the sauce: soak the tomatoes in the water for 30 to 60 minutes. Blend everything, including the water the tomatoes were soaking in, until smooth. If it's too thick, add more water or some mylk. If it's too thin, add more tahini and sun-dried tomatoes.

Mix the sauce with the cooked couscous, adding as much or as little as you like (I personally prefer not a lot of sauce), then garnish with the veggies, basil and mint.

> NOTE: If the sun-dried tomatoes you use already have salt added, there's no need to add salt to the sauce (unless you want to).

FULLY LOADED YAMS

with Black Beans, Sesame Miso Gravy, Green Onions + Purple Cabbage

Beeessssst.

2 large yams

TAHINI MISO GRAVY

⅓ cup (79 ml) water

3 tbsp (42 g) tahini

2 tbsp (30 ml) apple cider vinegar

1 heaping tbsp (14 g) miso paste

1 tsp maple syrup

1 peeled garlic clove

1 tsp chunk peeled ginger

2 cups (344 g) cooked black beans

⅓ cup (17 g) chopped green onions

⅓ cup (114 g) chopped purple cabbage

Preheat the oven to 350°F (177°C). Wash and scrub the yams then slice them in half lengthwise and bake with the cut-side down for 45 to 60 minutes, or until they are bubbling and tender all the way through (test with a fork). Mash a little space into each of them so you have a place to put the toppings.

To make the gravy: blend all the ingredients until smooth. If it's too thin, add more tahini. If it's too thick, add more water or apple cider vinegar.

Top off yams with the beans, green onions and cabbage, then drizzle with the gravy. Nom.

UDON NOODLE BOWL

with Miso Ginger Sauce, Edamame + Green Onions

Udon noodles are slightly thicker than others, and they have a satisfying chewy texture. When I stayed with my partner in a snowy mountain town last winter, we ate something similar to this every night and always wanted more.

2 ½ cups (230 g) uncooked whole grain, gluten-free udon noodles

2 cups (200 g) uncooked edamame

1 tbsp (14 g) chunk peeled ginger

1 large carrot

½ cup (118 ml) water, as needed

1 tsp maple syrup

2 tbsp (28 g) miso paste

¾ cup (37 g) chopped green onions

¼ tsp black pepper (optional)

Cook the noodles according to the package directions, but drain them a couple minutes before the directions say, and then rinse with cold water. Steam the edamame for 8 minutes, then shell all the soybeans out. Grate the ginger. Peel and slice the carrot into thin strips (like noodles) on a mandolin slicer or by hand.

In a frying pan over medium-high heat, add ¼ cup (59 ml) of the water and all the ginger, maple syrup and miso. When the water starts steaming and bubbling slightly, stir the miso around until it combines with the water. If you want to add more water, go ahead. Lower the heat and add the noodles and carrot strips. Stir everything together so it's evenly coated in the miso sauce. Take off the heat and add the soybeans and green onions.

Serve in bowls with a little black pepper on top, if you like.

CHANA MASALA

Quick Chickpea Curry with Rice

Not exactly made traditionally, but I'm impatient and often lazy, so this is what I do when I get that chana masala craving (which is everyday).

3 peeled garlic cloves

1 tbsp (14 g) chunk peeled ginger

⅓ cup (79 ml) water, or more as needed

3 tbsp (44 ml) fresh lemon juice

2 tsp (5 g) garam masala powder

1 (15-oz [425-g]) can chickpeas

1 (8-oz [227-g]) can tomato sauce

3 cups (483 g) cooked brown rice

¼ cup (12 g) basil leaves

Finely chop the garlic and ginger. In a frying pan over medium-high heat, add ¼ cup (59 ml) of the water and all the lemon juice and heat until they begin to steam and lightly bubble. Add the chopped garlic and ginger and sauté for 3 minutes, adding more water in 1 tablespoon (15 ml) amounts as needed for moisture if the pan starts getting dry. Throw on the garam masala powder and add more water if needed, stirring everything together. Next add the chickpeas and the tomato sauce and stir gently for 10 to 15 minutes on medium-low heat until the mixture has thickened up.

Serve with rice and garnish with basil.

EGGPLANT OREGANO STEAKS

with Lemony Broccolini + Spicy Chickpeas

When you add a little oil to eggplant and bake it, the result is a flavorful melt-in-your-mouth experience. Protein-rich chickpeas and tangy broccolini (aka baby broccoli) balance out this dish.

EGGPLANT STEAKS

1 large eggplant

2 to 4 tbsp (30 to 59 ml) extra virgin olive oil

2 tbsp (1 g) dried oregano

¼ tsp sea salt

LEMONY BROCCOLINI

¼ cup (59 ml) fresh lemon juice

1 tbsp (15 ml) maple syrup

1 tbsp (15 ml) gluten-free tamari

Water, if needed

3 cups (689 g) broccolini

SPICY CHICKPEAS

2 cups (328 g) cooked chickpeas

¼ tsp paprika powder

¾ tsp cumin powder

½ tsp ginger powder

¼ tsp black pepper

½ tsp turmeric powder

¼ tsp cinnamon powder

½ tsp dried oregano

1 to 2 tsp (5 to 9 ml) fresh lemon juice, as desired

To make the eggplant steaks: preheat the oven to 350°F (177°C). Wash the eggplant and slice it into ¾-inch (19-mm)-thick disks. Rub each disk thoroughly with oil, using as much as you need. Toss with oregano and salt and bake for 30 minutes or until tender all the way through (test with a fork).

To make the lemony broccolini: put all the ingredients into a frying pan over medium-high heat until the liquids are steaming. Cover and steam for 8 to 10 minutes or until the broccolini is vibrantly green and slightly tender. Check on the pan periodically to make sure the liquids haven't totally evaporated; if they do get low, add 1 tablespoon (15 ml) of water at a time as needed.

To make the spicy chickpeas: simply toss the chickpeas with the spices and lemon juice and adjust according to preference.

Serve everything on plates and enjoy.

RESOURCES

INGREDIENTS

Grab as much fresh produce from your local farmer's market as you can. It's gonna taste the best. Ask the vendors if they have any ugly produce they will sell for cheaper—also called "culled" produce—and when there's a good deal (e.g., beets for a buck a pound), load up and get creative with beets that week. To save money but still eat organic, check out the Environmental Working Group's Dirty Dozen and Clean Fifteen lists every year (just Google it); they tell you the most and least pesticide-contaminated foods. Buy the worst ones organic (like apples) and buy the least contaminated ones non-organic (like avocados). It's the perfect-ish happy medium.

The nuts you buy should be raw, unsalted and organic if possible. Get 'em from Prana if you're in Canada (hey, neighbor) by ordering from their site: boutiqueprana.com. If you're in the U.S., try nuts.com. Otherwise get nuts from your local health food store, though they might not be as fresh.

Let's talk oil. The best extra virgin olive oil is organic, sold in dark glass bottles and slightly cloudy with a few pieces of olive fragments still floating around in it. Buy this stuff if you can. Otherwise use organic olive oil for my cooked recipes because lower-quality extra virgin olive oil doesn't do well when heated.

Alternatively, use lemon juice or water instead of oil in all my recipes. Coconut oil should be raw, organic and unrefined. But if you despise the taste of coconut (I don't understand you people), go for the refined kind.

Some of you might be looking through the recipes and asking: what the frick is tamari (which begs a second question: why are you saying "frick")? I know it sounds strange, but it's basically just a better version of soy sauce. It has a deeper, more savory flavor, plus it's wheat-free and lower in salt. If you don't do soy, try this amazing thing called coconut aminos. It's also like soy sauce, but it comes from coconut, making it soy-free and gluten-free, and tastes SO GOOD. I would list it in every recipe, but it's a little expensive and even weirder-sounding than tamari.

I list a lot of whole-grain, gluten-free noodles, but I know in some regions these might be tricky to find. Look online and see if you can order them, or just use rice noodles, soba noodles or your fave gluten-free grain instead.

Beans should be organic and PLEASE look at the ingredients list if you are buying them canned—they put weird sh#t in there sometimes. The only ingredients should be beans, water and salt. A brand called Eden Organic uses kombu seaweed instead of salt, so they are the coolest, in my opinion. I usually use Eden Organic canned beans in my recipes because I am a lazy person, but I admit: cooking them yourself is probably worth it; it just takes a bit of time.

Apple cider vinegar should be unpasteurized (aka raw) and preferably organic. Bragg's is the brand to buy in the grocery store, unless you see some at the farmer's market.

Miso paste should be non-GMO, organic and unpasteurized as well. I know there are several different varieties of miso, but honestly I am not particular. Use your fave.

BOOKS

The China Study by Dr. Colin Campbell

Breaking the Food Seduction by Dr. Neal Barnard

Eat to Live by Dr. Joel Fuhrman

The Starch Solution by Dr. McDougall

Prevent and Reverse Heart Disease by Dr. Caldwell Esselstyn

Diet for a New America by John Robbins

Mad Cowboy by Howard Lyman

In Defense of Food by Michael Pollan

Eating Animals by Jonathan Safran Foer

DOCUMENTARIES

Forks Over Knives

Cowspiracy

Earthlings

Food Matters

Fat, Sick and Nearly Dead

BLOGS

This Rawsome Vegan Life (yours truly)

Sweetly Raw

Tales of a Kitchen

Happy. Healthy. Life.

Vegan Yack Attack

Keepin' It Kind

Post Punk Kitchen

Vegan Sidekick

The Dreamy Leaf

Faring Well

Earthsprout

The Simple Veganista

The First Mess

Vegan Richa

Coconut and Berries

Choosing Raw

Fettle Vegan

Vegan Miam

ACKNOWLEDGMENTS

Thanks to Page Street for making this third book happen! Will and Marissa, you're great. Thanks, mum and Jack, for being my hand models. Thanks, mum and dad, for just being. Thanks to all friends and family who tried these creations and gave me feedback, and the amazing volunteers who tested out my recipes in their own kitchens around the world and helped make them yummier. Thanks to the peeps who helped me narrow food photo options down to one (or two… UGH WHICH ONE!?) Thanks SO MUCH to everyone who reads my blog or has supported me in any way along this journey; I actually love you. Finally, thanks to Jack for basically eating everything in here and making me the happiest I've ever been. X

ABOUT THE AUTHOR

Emily von Euw lives in British Columbia, Canada. She is the creator of the award-winning food blog, This Rawsome Vegan Life (www.thisrawsomeveganlife.com) and author of the bestselling raw, vegan, gluten-free desserts cookbook, *Rawsome Vegan Baking*, and *100 Best Juices, Smoothies and Healthy Snacks*. When she is not writing cookbooks, making recipes for the blog or studying history at university she can be found singing out of tune to Mariah Carey in the forest, crying with joy when she thinks of baby pigs, devouring all sweet potatoes in sight and dancing the night away with friends (but often with just herself, like she did about 2 minutes ago).

INDEX

Z